I0759923

Philip Melancthon's

COMMENTARY ON ECCLESIASTES

Philip Melanchthon's Commentary on Ecclesiastes: An Unabridged Translation

All Scripture quotations are the translator's renderings of author's original translations.

Published by:
1517 Academic, an imprint of 1517.
PO Box 54032
Irvine, CA 92619-4032

Publisher's Cataloging-In-Publication Data
(Prepared by Cassidy Cataloguing, Inc.)

Names: Melanchthon, Philip, 1497-1560, author. | Cooper, Derek, 1978- translator.
Title: Philip Melanchthon's commentary on Ecclesiastes : an unabridged translation / Philip Melanchthon ; translated by Derek Cooper.
Other titles: Enarratio brevis conconium libri Salomonis cuius titulus est Ecclesiastes. English.
Description: Irvine, CA : 1517 Academic, an imprint of 1517, [2025] | Translation of: Enarratio brevis conconium libri Salomonis cuius titulus est Ecclesiastes. | Includes bibliographical references and index.
Identifiers: ISBN: 9781964419282 (hardcover) | 9781964419299 (ebook)
Subjects: LCSH: Bible. Ecclesiastes—Commentaries. | Theology. | Wisdom—Biblical teaching. | Mortality—Biblical teaching. | Providence and government of God—Biblical teaching. | BISAC: RELIGION / Biblical Commentary / Old Testament / Poetry & Wisdom Literature. | RELIGION / Christian Theology / History. | RELIGION / Biblical Commentary / General.
Classification: LCC: BS1475.53 .M4513 2025 | DDC: 223.807—dc23

Printed in the United States of America.

Cover art by Zachariah James Stuef.

Philip Melancthon's

COMMENTARY ON ECCLESIASTES

TRANSLATED BY

Derek Cooper

AN UNABRIDGED VERSION

Contents

Brief Commentary on the Sermons of the Book of Solomon Whose Title Is Ecclesiastes[1]

By Philip Melanchthon[2]

Philip Melanchthon Sends Greetings[3] *to the Renowned Gentleman, Lord Joachim Moller of Hamburg, Doctor of Law, Who Excels in Learning and Virtue.*[4]

---

[1] Philip Melanchthon, *Brief Commentary on the Sermons of the Book of Solomon Whose Title Is Ecclesiastes* (Wittenberg: Joseph Klug, 1550).

[2] The editorial comments on this commentary read as follows: "This book was transcribed in this way. It first appeared in Wittenberg before being recorded in 1550 by Joseph Klug in the year 1551. It was then reedited in Wittenberg in 1551 and then again in 1556 in which [Caspar] Peucer reprinted the same edition in the works of Melanchthon in Work II on page 915, from which we present this book. The dedicatory letter, addressed to Joachim Moller, we explained above that it dates to September 21, 1550. It was published in German under the care of Stephanus Riccius, student of Melanchthon: 'Ecclesiastes, interpreted by Philip Melanchthon, and printed by Stephan Reich [= Stephanus Riccius] in Wittenberg in 1561.'" See MBW 5908 for correction of date from October 1 to September 21.

[3] I am taking Melanchthon's use of "S. D." to mean *salutem dicit*, a common formula used in Latin letter writing.

[4] Joachim Moller the Younger (1521–1588) was a chancellor in the Principality of Lüneburg. His father, Joachim Moller the Elder, went by the same name. The addressee to the commentary, Moller the Younger, studied at the University of Wittenberg under the tutelage of Melanchthon, with whom

Having observed the saddest misfortunes of the human race at all times in history—the destruction of empires, the indiscriminate dissolution arising from human wickedness or from those whose morals were fractional at best and reproachful at worst—many have doubted whether divine providence rules over human affairs or whether all things in the world spin around by chance without the slightest design or natural motion, spiraling in a sort of aimless and inadvertent reeling.

In the face of such doubt, God opposes these accusations using testimonies about his own nature, namely, the very design of the world, the rotation of the planets, the evolution of time, the awe-inspiring creation of humankind, the ingenuity of the human mind, the understanding of order, the abiding ability to distinguish between that which is beautiful[5] and that which is base, the pangs of the conscience, the fruitfulness of the earth, the preservation of each species, and the punishment of heinous crimes. As if emerging from his mysterious throne, God has addressed the entire human race and preached human salvation and the coming judgment when he will make a universal and eternal distinction between the righteous and the wicked. In order that we would recognize these mysteries as true, he shows these things to be decreed by God by means of the resurrection of the dead, and in the many other awe-inspiring works.

And although precious few in the human race acknowledge these things, there always was and will be some Church of God—sometimes in larger numbers and other times in smaller ones—that embraces the divine message with hearty approval. This Church praises and worships the true God, teaches the chief causes of misfortunes lest, moved by the fickleness of fate, it would doubt the providence of God. And although, to be sure, dissimilar appearances are evident, we must nonetheless always discern in them the coming judgment [of God], knowing that the only standard in life is that which has

---

he stayed in correspondence his entire life. He subsequently moved to Italy to earn his Doctor of Law, which Melanchthon mentions here.

[5] For more on the German reformers and beauty, see Mark Mattes, *Martin Luther's Theology of Beauty: A Reappraisal* (Grand Rapids, MI: Baker Academic, 2017).

been divinely handed down in which it is necessary to acknowledge all human actions as falling under God's judgment and rule. The Church opposes this kind of doubt with the testimonies impressed in creation, the divine message handed down, and the examples of the resurrection of the dead and many similar things.

The godly are confirmed by the singular testimony in their hearts, which is never in doubt. For even when experiencing God's wrath, they acknowledge him to be truly angered by sin. And when once again they are raised up by faith in consolation, the flame in their chest brings forth light, they recognize that they are being brought back from hell, and they sense the beginning of eternal life. Concerning such testimony, Paul has said, "The Holy Spirit testifies with our spirit."[6]

No matter how much has been otherwise said by others about that argument in this book, I find comfort in the following thought—and I think the main part of this work is rightly organized in this way: that the whole sermon is doctrine, namely, it is an assertion concerning divine providence and a refutation of objections to it in which there are consolations and threats. For although great misfortunes occur in this life—such as the fact that unjust leaders who despise God rule empires, ungodly people flourish in their wealth, the Church is horribly persecuted for worshiping God in the right way, the voice of righteous teachers and wise advisers is often ignored, and a great deal of the human race is [spiritually] incurable—nevertheless, you must by no means suppose that there is no divine providence. On the contrary, the day of judgment is coming in which there will be an eternal distinction made between the good and the wicked.

Let's start with the consolations interwoven in this book in which arguments are drawn from the necessary, from the possible, and from the useful.[7] Because it is necessary to obey God, you fulfill the responsibilities of your calling regardless of the outcome. And these undertakings will never be in vain. For God will attend to the needs of the one who calls upon him, and God will be in control over that person's labors, dangers, and obstacles, just as the psalm says: "Commit your way to God. Hope in him and he will act [for

[6] Rom. 8:16.

[7] These are categories from ancient rhetoric.

you]."[8] This will not always be unpleasant labor since good things can sometimes happen. As Solomon says in this book, "Scatter your bread upon the waters, for you will find it again."[9] Just consider this image Solomon gives: He commands us to scatter healing doctrine and counsel as if we were scattering bread upon the waters, which we would otherwise assume would disintegrate there. But no—Solomon the Preacher promises us something better. He suggests that some part of your labors will be of benefit to the Church, to your home, and to your posterity even though you will not be able to establish that which was established by the likes of Joshua, Samuel, David, Solomon, or Josiah. However, you will be able to serve in your life station effectively just as Zechariah, Simeon, and those who came after them served in a wretched and oppressed land yet whose will was similar. Afterwards, even when unfavorable events happen to you, take rest in God so that you might know God and fulfill the responsibilities of your calling, which consist of being obedient to God in all circumstances, just as it has been written: "Humble yourselves under God's powerful hand."[10]

But it is not like today's circumstances. For God himself has already foretold that far greater fracturing in nations and the Church will occur in the very last days of the world than those that occurred in the days of the patriarchs and prophets [of the Old Testament]. And yet, each age bears witness to its own bitter examples. But now we are weighed down not only by the infirmities of this age but also by the weight of its punishments, which have piled up on account of so many idols and other crimes. And there is even greater madness in the devil since he can sense that the time of extreme judgment is at hand in which he knows for certain that greater torments are being set before him for all eternity.

And this leads Solomon to add the threats [found in this book]. Solomon hands down the following principle: Heinous crimes committed in this life will be punished. Nor are the unjust, he says, able to escape their just desserts.[11] In a related way, while the punishments

---

8 Ps. 37:5 (Vulgate 36:5).

9 Eccl. 11:1.

10 1 Pet. 5:6.

11 See Eccl. 8:8.

experienced in this life may vary, they will by no means be overlooked in the life to come. For example: "Although things will go well for those who fear God, they will certainly not go well for those who are godless. Indeed, their lives will not last forever but, instead, will be like a shadow fading into the darkness."[12]

Such are the primary topics in Solomon's sermon. And now, let the reader consider in himself how useful this doctrine is, which confirms in his mind such a teaching about [divine] providence and the coming judgment, which is the admonition of the responsibilities of our callings and a consolation regarding the difficulties arising from these events. For the first step in every serious deliberation should be the thought of providence, the judgment of God, and divine help.

The reader should be aware here also that these sermons are being read in the Church of God, where the doctrine of prayer to the true God and the redemption of the Son of God must be perceived and proclaimed. The recognition of the Son of God should outshine those labors about which this sermon speaks. And, in fact, Solomon himself commands here that the whole doctrine of the Church should be known and heard, and he rebukes useless worship, saying: "When you approach the house of God, enter with an ear toward obeying since obedience is better than the sacrifice of fools, for they do not know that they are doing evil."[13] You see here how seriously it is commanded that we hear doctrine in the house of God, that is, the sounding in the true Church, which embraces the entire doctrine from its foundation. For it was then necessary for the true God to be distinguished from the fictious gods of all the nations, and it was necessary that the promises concerning [Christ] the Redeemer be known and that the doctrine of the righteousness of faith be understood. There has not been, nor can there be now, any worship pleasing to God until the mind acknowledges the High Priest who bears our prayers and groanings to the Eternal Father.

Consequently, the prophets [of the Old Testament] taught that those who repent receive forgiveness of their sins, are reckoned as righteous, are filled with the Holy Spirit, and are adopted as heirs to eternal life through trust in [Christ] the Redeemer—not based

[12] Eccl. 8:11–13.

[13] Eccl. 5:1 (Vulgate 4:17).

on their own worth or the law. This knowledge of the Redeemer has shone forth in some prophets with more light and in others with less. As happens in every age, many even imagined that people are reckoned as righteous through pursuit of the law and that their sins are removed through animal sacrifice. Yet the [Old Testament] prophets, and many of their hearers, who rightly worshiped God, served as guardians of the true doctrine and faith [in Christ] the Redeemer.

And to the rest who thought they were appeasing God's wrath through sacrifices, Solomon says, "They do not know that they are doing evil."[14] In Solomon's succinct complaint here, we witness a sad reproach of the blindness of many who in all ages have been bewitched by a similar error. Similarly, there are many in our day "who do not know that they are doing evil" by establishing idols in the Mass and saying prayers for the dead. But it was necessary for them to hear the divine message, which reproaches errors and presents the proper way to pray to God.

I have been speaking briefly here about the basic argument of Solomon's book because it is beneficial for all to become intimately familiar with it, particularly those who teach literature. For the book truly contains many exceedingly useful admonitions that will aid both those who are current students as well as those who need to reread it. And although I saw that my commentary was quite meager, leading me to initially not want it to be published, I resisted this temptation since many thought that more people would be inclined to read the words of Solomon himself after I mentioned in my commentary how important the admonitions were that Solomon discussed in this book.

To this edition, I also attached your name because I know that in your civil service you, too, have frequently needed to refresh your spirit with these consolations, which assert that godly labors in government are pleasing to God and that they will not be done in vain even if one's good counsel is hindered in other ways. For there is no doubt that the devils plot against the human race, inciting some to attempt to destroy the Church by force and others to confuse it by sophistry and trickery. And upon these evils many other difficulties arise.

---

[14] Eccl. 5:1 (Vulgate 4:17).

Nevertheless, we know that the Son of God, "who sits at the right hand"[15] of the Eternal Father, is the guardian of his Church. Let us pray to him, requesting that he govern us, make us "vessels of mercy"[16] and "instruments of healing,"[17] assist our godly labors, support feeble Churches, and restrain the devil who attacks using tyranny and sophistry. We know that our prayers will not be in vain. Farewell and warm wishes. Written on September 21, 1550.

15 Rom. 8:34 and Heb. 1:3.

16 Rom. 9:23.

17 2 Tim. 2:20–21.

The Main Argument of Ecclesiastes

The arguments and aims of a writer are presented at the beginning of commentaries so that younger readers may be prepared forehand, may embrace and fix in their minds the main point of the work, and may consider to what use the written material is to be adapted, whether knowledge is the ultimate goal, or whether it may be useful for some activity in life.

Let us say something now as to writings in the Church. One part is doctrine, for instance, the recitation of the articles of faith. This is because God wants to be known by means of his revelations, he wants us to hear his message, and he wants us to come to recognize the clear testimonies that he has added to his message. God also wants us to agree with his words, going so far as to declare that this adherence is a virtue.

Knowledge, however, is not the ultimate goal. Instead, God wants us to add fear and consolation to knowledge since God ultimately revealed himself for this reason, namely, to collect for himself the Church Eternal out of the human race and to set it free from sin and death. Hearers, therefore, are to be raised up by this consolation on account of faith, which is the beginning of eternal life, and it is necessary to keep their minds and set their courses upon this consolation with the result that it yields [true] worship. Afterwards, they will enjoy the light, wisdom, goodness, and divine joy for all eternity, when "God will be all in all,"[1] that is, when God will be active in us

[1] 1 Cor. 15:28. Melanchthon began his lectures on 1 Corinthians in Wittenberg in the summer of 1521 and continued the following year with 2 Corinthians. In 1551 he provided lecture notes on the Corinthian correspondence for Paul

without the ministry of the Word but, instead, through his own light, we will see in plain sight.

Therefore, although some part of the writings of the Church is dogmatic or doctrinal, nevertheless, afterwards those other ends are to be examined. For just as a learned preacher recites at one time and in an orderly fashion creedal articles or the law, at another time he presents threats, accusing the guilty, to arouse in their minds the fear of divine judgment. At still other times, the preacher also proclaims the message of the Gospel and the consolations that the Son of God, our Lord Jesus Christ, handed down to the Church. The preacher thereby kindles faith and worship, and he soothes our sorrow lest our hearts are crushed by despair, and we fall into ruin.

In this way, let the preacher know that the parts of his sermon are to be distributed in this way, as Paul himself advised: "Devote yourself to reading, teaching, and exhortation."[2] First, let the godly preacher read the books of the prophets and apostles. Second, let him take up the things of the Church that must be presented without inventing new opinions or fictitious teachings, such as what Numa Pompilius[3] and others did. Indeed, a godly preacher must present those things taken [directly] from the fountainhead with clarity and without corruption, teaching about definitions and distinctions elsewhere. The latter fall under the office of teacher. And finally, a godly preacher is to communicate his teaching in such a way that it arouses Fear and Faith, which is the consolation and restoration of life.

But after the reader of Solomon's sermons has considered that these are the counsels of the writers, let him know that this entire book—whose title is *Ecclesiastes*—consists primarily of teaching, namely, it is a strong assertion about providence. Solomon confirms that God is wise, true, just, a judge, and a completely free agent. This

---

Eber, who published them in 1561 as *Brevis et utilis Commentarius in priorem epistolam Pauli ad Corinthios, et in aliquot capita secundae, scriptus a Philippo Melanthone* (Wittenberg: Crato, 1561). See CR 15:1053–1220.

[2] 1 Tim. 4:13.

[3] Numa Pompilius (753-673 BCE) was a Roman king who supposedly succeeded the mythical founder of Rome, Romulus. Many religious institutions and practices are attributed to him, hence Melanchthon's reference to his role in establishing pagan worship in Rome.

God is to be worshipped according to the teaching handed down by God himself and by no one else. God will punish those who despise him while nonetheless showing mercy and salvation to those who call upon him and begin to obey him. In this way, the primary aim of this book is dogmatic in nature [δογματική]: to offer an assertion of providence against the Epicureans, Skeptics, Stoics, and other freethinkers of thought that undermines belief in providence. And, in fact, there are clear assertions in these words from the last chapter. For instance: "God will bring all things under judgment; he will judge all things now hidden—both the good and the evil."[4] Solomon also writes in Chapter 11, "But know that for all these things, God will bring you into judgment."[5] Likewise in Chapter 3: "God will judge both the righteous and the unrighteous."[6] In these and similar words, may you understand that the main proposition of this whole sermon [of Ecclesiastes] is read and repeated.

The teaching of obedience then follows this assertion. When God gave the law and added threats, he also mercifully offered the message of the Gospel concerning reconciliation as well as the most magnificent promises while nonetheless punishing with certainty those who despise him. But God will receive and preserve those who flee to the Son, the Mediator. It is necessary for such people to obey God according to God's teaching, that there may be fear in their hearts out of reverence for God's judgment, and that there may be faith resting in the Mediator. This faith establishes that we are received, heard, helped, protected, and preserved by him. And, finally, be sure to restrain the members of your body lest they lead you to violate the commands of God. Accordingly, teaching is transferred to practice when obedience follows assent to providence, and in that obedience our hearts are sustained by divine consolation and freed from eternal death. This is when life in heaven begins, which we must recognize as the ultimate goal.

But in this assertion of providence there seem to be many misfortunes in life that stand against us. To be sure, the Just Judge, as far as possible, defends the just, restrains those who want to do unjust

4 Eccl. 12:14.

5 Eccl. 11:9.

6 Eccl. 3:17.

things, and punishes those who have offended him. In the human race, however, many of the just lie crushed by great hardships. For instance, how many thousands of innocent children, young women, and wives perish every day in wars, fires, and other calamities. Meanwhile, the wicked are not only not punished, but they seem to flourish, lead kingdoms, and possess wealth. Such a confusing reality causes us to ponder whether God actually rules over our lives. This complaint is found in the writings of many people, as is well known, and it appears in writings of all kinds. And, indeed, there is no person alive who will not be tormented by this question.

Even worse, it seems like both the good and the wicked die equally in the most meaningless of ways, as if they were violets trampled in the mud or leaves blown to the ground by the wind. Indeed, more often than not, it appears that the endeavors of the wise and the righteous are in vain just as those of the wicked result in victory. Still, even when Nebuchadnezzar was laying waste to all of Judea through the destruction of Jerusalem and nearby towns, the True Church survived among the Jewish people. This spectacle caused many in the nation of Israel to no longer believe that God cared for them. And although there are many examples of God's presence in nature and in the preservation of the human race—for instance, in the orderly motions of the heavenly bodies, the mind's capacity for knowledge, the preservation of the species, and the regular punishment of savage crimes—it is not easy to simply dismiss the Epicureans, who build a case against divine providence by collecting these spectacles of confusions. But Solomon opposes this kind of reasoning by offering steadfast and true answers that are not born from human reason but that, instead, present the very voice of God concerning the coming judgment after this life.

For example, Solomon writes in Chapter 8 that many crimes will be punished even in this life: "Just as battle cannot be escaped during times of war, so the ungodly cannot be saved by practicing ungodliness."[7] However, Solomon then admits that judgment may be deferred for some time, lamenting that this brief delay of punishment can embolden the brazenness of criminals. But he opposes such criminal acts with the eternal life to come. Our present life is a

[7] Eccl. 8:8.

brief shadow. And in it neither punishment nor joy endure forever. In contrast, that which is eternal—whether eternally good or eternally wicked—is not a fleeting shadow. Solomon commands all of us to ponder this eternity and to take heed that we do not fall under God's eternal wrath where horrible and unceasing torment lies in wait. He also commands us to ask for and expect eternal blessings. Solomon responds that faith brings comfort to those who have converted to God, for faith escaped God's wrath and asks and expects eternal salvation. As a result, faith obeys and sustains itself in the knowledge of God's [eternal] presence and of divine assistance in the midst of present hardships. Now, the Church also knows that it has been burdened in this life with a mass of miseries. And though there is no doubt that Epicurus would laugh at Solomon's response, a godly mind assents to and believes in God's assurance concerning future judgment.

Consequently, this sermon of Solomon is prophetic, and it offers a divine message for the Church of God concerning future judgment, as does the Son of God's sermon in Matthew 25 and in many other places [in Scripture]. As a result, this book of Solomon is not to be read like the letters of Crates or Seneca,[8] which condemn riches, or like writings scolding monks for fleeing society. Rather, Solomon's book presents the teaching of faith concerning the judgment of God and the distinction between the ungodly and the Church, and, among the horrible misfortunes of the human race, Solomon presents the wrath of God to the defiant and consolation to the godly. Consequently, Solomon provides a long commentary about misfortunes and scandals with the ultimate purpose of teaching that we are by no means to judge from such scandals what God's will is in this life; rather, we are to assent to the divine message with a steadfast faith and recognize that the word of God is the standard [*norma*] of all our plans and actions, just as it has been written: "Your word is a lamp to my feet."[9]

In reading this book, it is necessary to have in mind the sum of Church teaching concerning the creation of the world, the creation

---

[8] Crates of Thebes (365-285 BCE) was a Greek cynic philosopher, while Seneca (4 BCE–65 CE) was a Roman stoic philosopher. See especially the latter's *Ad Lucillium epistulae morales.*

[9] Ps. 119:105 (Vulgate 118:105).

of humankind, the fall of humankind, the causes of this calamity, the promise [of redemption], and the Mediator by whom and through whom the Church is again gathered, along with faith that receives the forgiveness of sins, the law of God, eternal life, the judgment, the eternal punishments of the ungodly, and, finally, salvation of the godly.[10] When there is a discussion of providence, it is necessary to consider the entire teaching [of the Church]. And because the widespread confusions in this short life are able to cast doubt in our minds with the result that we are less able to discern providence, it is necessary to ponder the next life—the one that exists for eternity—and in which there will be a very clear distinction between the good and the wicked.

Let us now turn to the different divisions in this book of Solomon. Solomon first recites the objections that seem to be opposed to providence. And in this recitation, he speaks at length about the great and constant upheavals in society that secular thinking loves to ensnare in our minds. As a result, this part of the book is quite lengthy, though Solomon sprinkles succinct axioms from time to time, such as "fear God,"[11] since we must be mindful of future judgment. We must embrace these very succinct axioms with steadfast assent and faith. Indeed, it is most certain that these divine decrees are often repeated in the Church by means of the voice of the prophets, Christ, and the apostles, for a confident faith and succinct divine sayings [such as these] stand in opposition to the distressing thoughts that sometimes wreak havoc in our minds. In fact, this very method of offering an objection and then the answer imitates the internal battles of human reason itself.

Now follows Solomon's assertation of providence, the Law, and threat but, likewise, the Gospel and consolation. After it has been determined that God is both a judge and a vindicator, you must pay heed to the commandments [that God has given] and obey them. In fact, there are many obstacles to obeying God, since both the [spiritual] infirmity inherent in humanity and the madness of the devils, who generate mass confusion among the human race, are very great.

[10] Here Melanchthon gives a list similar to his own *Loci communes*, the German version of which he published in 1555.

[11] The direct phrase "fear God" only appears in Eccl. 12:13, which many scholars understood as a conclusion to the book.

As such, comfort is necessary here. Consequently, the message of the Gospel must be heard, which teaches what obedience is and how it may be pleasing [to God]. This voice of the Gospel orders governmental leaders not to abandon their duties even though, in the chaos of this life, good decisions do not always meet with good outcomes. It also orders us not to be broken by despair even though the unrighteous flourish for longer than we want, and, meanwhile, the true Church is oppressed. That is because even though God's judgment is deferred for a while, criminals will be punished later: both in this life and in all eternity.

The consolation is often interwoven with this writing, which is also included in all of Psalm 37, namely, "Do not fret,"[12] and in many other sermons preached by the prophets and the Son of God. For instance, the Son of God preaches in Matthew 10: "Do not fear those who kill the body but cannot kill the soul; rather, fear the one who can destroy both soul and body in hell."[13] Eternity is, by far, to be preferred rather than the briefest span of this mortal life, and yet, in this life, terrible punishments may follow savage offenses. For instance: "Whoever draws the sword will die by the sword."[14] Indeed, experience has borne these words to be true: "The one who devises evil for another, devises it for one's own self."[15] For instance, consider King Archelaus of Macedonia.[16] Although he was an outstanding king for a while, he was ultimately assassinated by his own people because he had seized the kingdom by means of a crime. And there are many other such examples in history.

In this way, the reader, not at all unskilled in common life, can easily understand what the use of this book of Solomon is and what is to be gained from it. In short, Solomon the Preacher's

---

[12] Ps. 37:1. Of course, in the text itself, Melanchthon refers to this as Psalm 36 since he is using the Latin Vulgate version.

[13] Matt. 10:28.

[14] Matt. 26:52.

[15] This quote appears to be in both Hesiod's *Works and Days* [line 57] and Callimachus's *Aetia* [fragment 2.5]. The text in Greek is as follows: τεύχων ὡς ἑτέρῳ τὶ, ἑῷ κακὸν ἥπατι τεύχει.

[16] Archelaus was king of Macedonia from 413 to 399 BCE. It was believed that Archelaus seized control of Macedonia illegally after murdering several in the royal family: his half-brother, uncle, and cousin.

assertion about providence in these sayings, which are proposed in the Church not by human authority but by God, must be affirmed. And, consequently, each person must obey God in his station and perform the duties of his vocation. And although, to be sure, there will be many obstacles that arise when attempting to do so, each person must cling to the consolations that Solomon sets forth here. Each person must come to know how he may please God, that God is the ultimate ruler over the assembly, that God wants us to seek out divine aid and sincerely offer help to those who serve in their vocations faithfully and, finally, that the Church is to be united into an eternal union with the Godhead, in which "God will be all in all."[17] By this faith, may each person obey God, do what is right[eous], submit to God without complaint, remain faithful to the duties of his vocation even when in despair, and not fall into the contempt of God like an Epicurean.

Having considered this admonition about the use of this book, your reading of it will now be clearer and sweeter, and, in fact, almost the entirety of this work is contained in these deliciously sweet rules of life. As Psalm 37 says: "Be subject to God and pray to him."[18] And: "Commend your way to God, hope in him, and he will do this."[19] And also: "Hope in the Lord and keep his way."[20] And Psalm 55 says, "Cast your cares on the Lord and he will sustain you."[21] And Matthew 6 states, "But seek first God's kingdom, and everything else will be added to you. And do not worry about tomorrow, for each day has enough trouble of its own."[22] That is, do that which is necessary and ask and expect help from God lest you be upset by trivial matters. But in observing the commandments of God, you will do well to follow this norm and to glean from the Gospel that obedience to [Christ] the Mediator is most pleasing, and that all your labors done through him and by him will prosper. For as the Mediator said, "Without me, you

---

[17] 1 Cor. 15:28.

[18] Ps. 37:7. Of course, in the text itself, Melanchthon refers to this as Psalm 36 since he is using the Latin Vulgate version.

[19] Ps. 37:5.

[20] Ps. 37:34.

[21] Ps. 55:22 (Vulgate 54:23).

[22] Matt. 6:33–34.

can do nothing."[23] And Paul wrote, "Nothing you do in the Lord is ever in vain."[24] That is because the Son of God himself will guarantee that your course will benefit the Church, as it is written: "When he ascended, he gave gifts to his people, for instance, prophets, apostles, teachers," and so on.[25] And, finally, it is said in the psalm: "God offers deliverance to kings."[26]

Those with sound minds understand that these consolations are true and beneficial. And because a great part of these consolations belongs to the virtue that is called "Patience,"[27] I will briefly discuss this admonition at the beginning. First, it is important to distinguish philosophical patience from Christian patience. Philosophical patience means to obey reason even in the inevitable difficulties and hardships that reason commands us to bear, to do nothing against justice, and to find consolation in our grief only by what our conscience deems right. In this way, philosophical patience offers no hope of aid since reason offers neither assistance nor comfort before death. This was the case with Aristides and Camillus,[28] both of whom suffered injuries in exile with a calm mind, yet without the faintest expectation of divine assistance.

By contrast, Christian patience obeys God even in the midst of the inevitable difficulties and hardships we bear, and which God commands us to bear, both doing nothing against justice and requesting and expecting assistance and comfort from God by means of [Christ] the Mediator. And such confidence in God's presence offers us consolation in our grief. For instance, we witness in David, Jeremiah, and

---

[23] Jn. 15:5.

[24] 1 Cor. 15:58.

[25] This is a partial quotation from Eph. 4:8 and 11, but, of course, Melanchthon routinely evokes an entire *locus*, or series of verses, rather than just one.

[26] Ps. 144:10.

[27] It is important to note that, in Latin, *patientia* can be translated in numerous ways: "suffering," "endurance," "forbearance," and "patience." I opted for "patience," since suffering is not a "virtue," but the etymology of the word hearkens back to "suffering."

[28] Marcus Furius Camillus (c. 446-365 BCE) was a Roman soldier and statesman who, despite victories for Rome, was banished, while Aristides (530-468 BCE) was a statesman in Athens active during the Persian War.

in others how the virtues of faith and hope are always linked to obedience; and these virtues of faith and hope produce joy in our hearts. As Paul says, "We have been justified by faith."[29] Likewise: "May the peace of God preserve your hearts."[30] To this belongs the Pauline rule written to the Thessalonians: "Rejoice always, pray without ceasing, and give thanks in all circumstances."[31] But in order for this faith to be kindled in our hearts, it is [first] necessary to know the Gospel concerning forgiveness of sins and reconciliation by means of the Mediator, the Son of God, our Lord Jesus Christ. Faith looks to him and knows that we are led to the Eternal Father through him. For this faith knows that Mediator is the shelter by which we are protected lest we be consumed by the horrible wrath of God or lest the devils be able to exercise their fury against us as they desire. Faith knows that the Church is only able to be protected and preserved by the Mediator, the Son of God. This confidence in the Mediator should shine forth in the performance of all our actions, as is often said at great length.

I will omit long recordings about how this book of Solomon has been obscured in other people's interpretations. In brief, some interpretations sought a scientific explanation, while others were fanatical, arguing that this book rejected marriage, government, the necessary work of the Church, authority, and economic order[32]—and thus, commanding everyone to abandon their vocation. However, it is necessary at the beginning to be warned that these monkish ravings must be rejected. Solomon most certainly does not reject God's own creatures or people's vocations. On the contrary, Solomon commands us to make use of them with reverence and order. What Solomon rejects is the perversion of order devised in the human heart that is so influenced by unfortunate events in our lives that it musters the temerity to doubt God's providence. But since false interpretations of this book have thrown great darkness on the teaching of the Gospel, it is useful for a younger generation to be reminded of more sensible thoughts.

---

29 Rom. 5:1.

30 Col. 3:15.

31 1 Thess. 5:16–18.

32 Melanchthon is referring here to the "three estates": *oeconomia, politia, ecclesia.*

For, unfortunately, a false interpretation of the following saying has been disseminated in the Church: "No one knows whether they are worthy of love or hate."[33] According to false interpretations, this saying is supposedly contrary to the sentiment of Solomon's book, implying that we will always doubt whether we can please God. However, the truth of the matter is that Solomon wants to cure such doubt. Indeed, Jeremiah and other believers did not doubt whether they were pleasing in God's sight even after seeing their homeland being burned to the ground and their people being carried into exile. For Solomon wishes this very thing about the will of God to be judged according to his Word, not judged from adverse circumstances occurring in this life. At any rate, I have said enough about the argument of this book.

[33] Eccl. 9:1. This text was used by Wittenberg's Roman opponents, who used it to prove that no one should claim to be sure about their relation to God but instead, out of humility, not be certain whether they were saved.

Ecclesiastes 1

[Ecclesiastes 1:1]

"The words of the Preacher, the son of David, the king of Jerusalem."[1]

In the title [of the work], the author calls himself Solomon, King, and Ecclesiast, that is, "Preacher," a name that refers to the office of rulers whose duty it is to ensure that Churches are to be taught rightly, as it is said in Psalms: "And, now kings, understand."[2] Likewise: "Open your gates, princes."[3] Also: "When the kings and the people come together as one to serve the Lord…"[4] It was proper for both rulers and the general public to think often about this sweet verse since it was commanded to each of them in order to come together, that is, in order to preserve the common assembly and ministry of the divine message, thereby learning true teaching, truly invoking God in unity, and mightily endeavoring to preserve this teaching. Moreover, of such godly unity, kings ought to be both commanders and authors of it. Therefore, Solomon, too, calls himself in this verse a "Preacher," signifying that he wants to be the author of godly unity in the Church as well as the preserver of true teaching.

---

1 Eccl. 1:1.

2 Ps. 2:10.

3 Ps. 24:7 (Vulgate 23:7).

4 Ps. 102:22 (Vulgate 101:23).

[1:2–4]

"Vanity of vanities! Everything is vanity. What more does a person have from all his labor?"[5]

First of all, you must know that this saying should not be interpreted as stating that things are bad [by necessity]; on the contrary, the following saying from Genesis must be firmly preserved: "God saw all that he had made, and it was very good," that is, all things were established by God's wisdom and goodness, which was in keeping with God's wisdom, those very things being pleasing to God and having been created for those very uses that preserve nature. From the beginning, it is necessary to be quite mindful of this interpretation. In fact, while Genesis speaks about things that were created and kept in their own order, Solomon speaks about human affairs. Solomon also strategically employs the phrase "under the Sun"[6] in order to signify that he does not include God, the Word of God, or the ministries of God in any way whatsoever under the concept of vanity, since these latter [two] are ruled by the Word of God. For, indeed, these things also, when they retain their own order, are good things. Instead, what is being spoken about here is the distortion of order, that is, Solomon speaks about things and matters that have been compared to the human heart since it mixes together confusions of order. Therefore, Solomon says, "All things are vain…that are under the Sun,"[7] a statement which encompasses all human affairs, consigning them to be fleeting, transitory, fickle, full of suffering, resistant to everlasting peace of mind, without pleasure, without riches, without wisdom and human virtue, without glory, and without any great amount of authority. Concerning all these things and matters, many

---

[5] Eccl. 1:2–3. The Latin word *vanitas* is capable of various translations. Although I have stuck with the traditional translation of this word from the book, *vanitas* could be accurately translated as "emptiness," "meaningless," "nothingness," "untruth," "fickleness," "deception," etc.

[6] Eccl. 1:3. Keep in mind that, even though Melanchthon did not directly quote this part of the verse above, his abbreviated citation encompasses the entire *locus* of the verses.

[7] Eccl. 1:2–3.

great miseries are united on account of human weakness. In this way, only the mercy of God, which is recognized in God's promises, brings about steadfast and everlasting peace and joy in our hearts.

At the same time, I did mention in the beginning that this book is one of comfort. Therefore, the other part of the book's subject matter offers a lament that records miseries and affirms that our spirits cannot find rest in [fleeting] things or human affairs. As such, these matters or circumstances are not to be given preference over the Word of God. Therefore, the Antithesis has been added, which contains the other part of the book's subject matter as well as the main argument of the work [of Ecclesiastes]. And here it is: Let the Word of God govern our minds, regardless of a situation's outcome. In this way, let our minds surrender to God, just as Paul commanded: "Let the peace of Christ rule in your hearts."[8]

[1:5-11]

"The Sun rises and sets and returns to its place... All streams run to the sea..."[9]

Solomon now employs an image taken from the motions of the Sun and waters, the application of which must be carefully considered. For this image of fluctuation and orbiting[10] is only presented for the purpose of drawing a comparison to human affairs, signifying that misfortunes are not able to be thwarted by human wisdom or human counsel. For instance, great rebellions and repeated insurrections occurred in the Roman Republic[11] under commanders and tribunes,

---

[8] Col. 3:15.

[9] Eccl. 1:5–7. As usual, Melanchthon only cites parts of verses, but intends all of it to be included in his *locus*.

[10] Melanchthon was aware of the heliocentric view, as Nicolaus Copernicus's *On the Revolutions of the Celestial Spheres* was published in 1543. However, Melanchthon still held to a geocentric view, believing the Sun revolved around the Earth.

[11] The Roman Republic is traditionally dated to have lasted from 509 to 27 BCE, followed by the Roman Empire.

later causing a monarchy to be desired; nonetheless [after being established], the same misfortunes returned.

Similarly, in Israel, when so many great calamities had befallen the rulers before the time of the monarchy, the people wanted the monarchy to be established and longed for the direction of the nation to be changed into something better and more stable. Nevertheless, there only followed even greater divisions. Therefore, when human societies are unstable and do not bring about peace and quiet, you are to do what is necessary and to take solace in God. As such, the most straightforward way to understand this verse's imagery is as follows: Just as the Sun and water maintain constant rotations and are constantly revolving, in the same way, human affairs, which have been mixed together with misfortunes, are also in a constant state of revolution; neither counsel nor human wisdom is able to thwart the calamities completely.

Oftentimes, whether in private or in public matters, we seek to adopt other forms of counsel in order to bring about a better state of affairs; but, nonetheless, the same misfortunes ensue. Solomon says in this *locus*, "There is nothing new under the Sun."[12] And afterward, he adds the reason for this: "The perverse are hard to correct, and the number of fools is infinite,"[13] which is to say that no human wisdom is capable of preventing or avoiding all stumbling and unfortunate accidents. That's because human nature is weak and foolish; thus, those things that occurred in previous times occur in all times and, subsequently, in the [entire] human race. And by this assertion one is able to understand that this description in the text represents a lament, that is, it is a description of human misfortune recurring in a similar way. As Thucydides said, "Similar things will continue to occur as long as the nature of humankind remains the same. Based on the [specific] circumstances, some will occur somewhat milder and others somewhat crueler."[14]

This consideration is necessary so that we, being forewarned, may prepare ourselves for the coming of adverse circumstances,

---

[12] Eccl. 1:10.

[13] Eccl. 1:15.

[14] Thucydides, *History of the Peloponnesian War* 3.82. Thucydides is describing when the people of Corcyra turned upon themselves and began killing each other, laying bare the depravity of human nature.

with the result that we should come to know our need to seek aid from God and find solace in God, for it is God who through prayers diminishes calamities both in the Church and privately. Incidentally, those who are learned should observe this saying affirming that "the Earth remains while the Sun is moved."[15] However, I will lay aside additional scientific disputes.[16]

[1:12-15]

"I, the Preacher, was king in Jerusalem," etc.[17]

To begin with, it is important to note here that Solomon is not speaking about a scientific consideration [of everything under heaven] in which, if the observation of order and design in the work of the world were shrewdly undertaken, would offer clear evidence about God and Providence. Rather, Solomon is speaking from the perspective of [human] Wisdom, that is, from considering plans, actions, and outcomes in human affairs, whether political or economic. Therefore, Solomon expressly says that he had considered those things that are under the Sun, that is, plans and outcomes of human actions, just as Pericles, Demosthenes, and Cicero are wise statesmen. Solomon is speaking here about such wisdom. He interprets this very wisdom or contemplation from government affairs to be an evil affliction, adding that it was given by God to human beings. Such things seem futile, but first the vocation, wisdom, or governance of Pericles or Cicero must be discerned. Although the vocation is good and has been established by God, the so-called wise governance of Pericles demonstrated an evil affliction on two accounts: first, in that Pericles frequently erred in his plans and, second, it was also often the case that situations [in which he found himself] did not correspond with good plans.

This, therefore, produced affliction, that is, punishment or suffering, in line with Demosthenes's saying that, if he could live his life

---

15 Eccl. 1:4.

16 Note that Melanchthon is referring to the heliocentric view, recently popularized by Copernicus, mentioned in the footnote above.

17 Eccl. 1:12

over, he would rather go directly to death than enjoy the highest honors.[18] Similarly, Aeschines said that he would rejoice in the prospect of fleeing from governing as a person being set free from a rabid dog.[19] Therefore, all prudent rulers and governors realize that government is not only full of cares, but it is also full of impediments, errors, and sorrowful events, all of which greatly torment our lives. Hence, we see the source of all those poems devised about Prometheus being bound to the Caucasus Mountains,[20] Sisyphus and the rolling boulder,[21] and similar ones.

Now, someone may then ask the following: "Was this affliction given by God?" Here is my reply: Speaking in generalities, it is true that God wills forth punishment; however, it by no means follows that God is the cause of sin.[22] For instance, God wanted Nero to be punished; nevertheless, God never drove Nero to commit any of his horribly evil deeds and instead allowed Nero to fall [on his own accord]. In this way, the clear response is that God allows leaders to make mistakes and allows for hindrances and unfortunate events to transpire in order to punish human arrogance. Likewise, God also allows such events in order to admonish some lest all others become overtaken by selfish desire, ambition, or [vain] curiosity. Rather than these, one's mind is supposed to be governed in its calling by the Word of God, and inside of these limits a person is to be restricted, seeking and anticipating further actions from God and also obeying God in the face of dismal events. For instance, Josiah waged an unnecessary war against Egypt. Pericles, likewise, entered battle due to the restlessness in his spirit and in his pride. And Marius went to war out of ambition. All these men erred in their plans.

---

[18] Location of quote unknown.

[19] Location of quote unknown.

[20] According to Greek mythology, Prometheus was bound to the Caucasus Mountains for teaching humans about fire and the arts. This story is most notably told in Aeschylus's play *Prometheus Bound*.

[21] According to Greek mythology, Sisyphus was punished by the gods for cheating death. His punishment was rolling a giant boulder up a hill every day only for it to return to the bottom, forcing him to roll it up again. This story is told by numerous ancient authors, including Homer, Plato, and Ovid.

[22] This was a common accusation of Catholics against Lutherans.

Nevertheless, it is not always the case that good advice produces good outcomes. For instance, the Israelites oftentimes had the regrettable experience of [losing even when] fighting a completely just cause—such as the time they were defeated by the Benjaminites[23]—because God wanted both parties to be punished. In this way, God wishes to offer instruction lest we, becoming overly confident in our own wisdom or power, undertake that which is not necessary. Likewise, he wants to teach us that when we do that which is necessary we must remain humble, acknowledging that we deserve whatever punishment may follow. At the same time, he wants to teach us that by faith we should ask and anticipate good outcomes from God. In a related way, we are to obey God even when God punishes us and gives us outcomes that we do not want. Indeed, as this entire passage is stating, such affliction has been divinely imposed upon the entire human race since to be human is to suffer and since punishment follows the depravity of nature and the commission of many sins.

[1:16–18]

"I have spoken in my heart," etc.
"My mind has wisely contemplated many things," etc.
Because in much wisdom there is much displeasure,
and the one adding wisdom adds pain."[24]

As I said above, Solomon is not offering a scientific discourse on the order and design of the world nor of the knowledge of the Word of God. Rather, Solomon is speaking from the perspective of human plans, actions, and outcomes in which we recognize that one's entire life is marked by troubles, errors, vices, and calamities. Those who are wise and experienced in governing are able to discern near and present evils as well as being able to calculate future disasters and

---

[23] Melanchthon is most likely referring to the battles between the Benjaminites and Israelites recorded in Judges 20.

[24] Eccl. 1:16 and 1:18. Although Melanchthon did not explicitly quote all the verses (and every word in the verses), his abbreviated citation encompasses the entire *locus* of verses 16 to 18.

many unpleasant occurrences from present situations. As a result, they are afflicted with great pain on account of present and future sufferings. Indeed, from a single set of changes that occur follow greater troubles, as in the case of the war embarked upon by Pericles, from which followed the ruin of nearly all the greatest cities in Greece. And nothing is truer than what Pindar said: "It is easy for God to move a city wherever God wishes, but to remain at peace is only from God."[25]

In summary, this is the lament that Solomon offers in this chapter, and, although consolation will eventually follow, he does not add any here. This chapter can be summarized as follows: In this life, we witness many troubles, great mistakes, and many heartbreaking events. Therefore, we cannot find peace in such things since such misfortune does not bring about the peace we long for, nor are we to withdraw from God when these misfortunes strike. Instead, we are to obey God patiently, to look in anticipation of God's protection and liberation, and to find peace in God by faith according to God's Word. In fact, this is not just a summary of this first chapter, but of the entire book [of Ecclesiastes], which perfectly aligns with the following sayings: "Be subject to God and pray to him,"[26] and "Caste your care upon God and he will sustain you."[27] Solomon waits until the third chapter and the ones that follow before adding this consolation.

---

[25] Pindar, *Pythian* 4.272. Pindar was a Greek poet who lived from 518 to 438 BCE. The Greek original to Melanchthon's Latin quotation is: ῥᾴδιον μὲν γὰρ πόλιν σεῖσαι καὶ ἀφαυροτέροις ἀλλ᾽ ἐπὶ χώρας αὖτις ἕσσαι δυσπαλὲς δὴ γίγνεται, ἐξαπίνας εἰ μὴ θεὸς ἁγεμόνεσσι κυβερνατὴρ γένηται. A rough translation of this is, "It is easy for even the weak to shake a city; however, it is, indeed, difficult to establish it in its place again unless God were to suddenly take the helm and help the rulers."

[26] Ps. 37:7 (36:7 in Vulgate).

[27] Ps. 55:22 (54:23 in Vulgate).

Ecclesiastes 2

[2:1-3]

"I said in my heart, 'I will go, I will abound in pleasure, and I will enjoy the good things.' But then I saw that this, too, was vanity."

Themistocles, Lucullus, and many others ultimately gave themselves over to the pleasures of their [morally] disintegrating society because of the countless useless rivalries and collective ingratitude that characterized those societies. Thus, human nature slides from one extreme to another, indulging profusely in pleasure as it grows bored of its labors. Solomon here also labels this kind of seeking after tranquility "vanity." However, this is not a rebuke of pleasure in and of itself. On the contrary, God himself, in his incredible goodness, has established this life to be one full of many sweet pleasures. For example, food, drink, and many other things have been established by God to be enjoyed when received with prayer and thanksgiving. However, vanity rears its head when one desires to enjoy pleasures in and of themselves rather than enjoying them in God.

Moreover, there is much pain that accompanies these pleasures, with such laments appearing frequently among the poets. For instance, Ovid says, "There is no genuine pleasure. For every happiness is tainted by some grief."[1] Likewise, Plautus states, "Is it not the case that the pleasures in life are short in proportion to their pains?"[2] Also: "Sorrow accompanies pleasures like a partner."[3] This

[1] Ovid, *Metamorphoses* 7.453–4.

[2] Plautus, *Amphitryon* 2.2.

[3] Plautus, source unknown.

is what Solomon meant when he wrote, "I understood laughter to be foolishness,"[4] namely, that the pleasures of the body are neither enduring nor essential. Nor is a different opinion to be sought elsewhere. Instead, what this passage signifies is that people may not find rest in the pleasures of the body not to be overcome by them lest they abandon God inasmuch as these pleasures have a tendency to obstruct and steal [true repose]. For, as Solomon earlier advised, we must not abandon God just because unfortunate and troubling events happen in our society. Rather, we must patiently obey God and anticipate from God good things.

[2:4–6]

"I made my works great, I built homes for myself, I planted vineyards," etc.

What follows here is a lament about a related pleasure, namely, that of pursuing extravagance and splendor in this life and showing undue interest in the acquisition of many things. Such a desire is no trifling matter because it leads to neglecting that which is necessary in exchange for seeking with great care and attention that which is not.

[2:7–26]

"I possessed male and female servants, I had a large family," etc.

Solomon presents some additional matters in this section, such as diligence in performing domestic responsibilities, which are sometimes full of drudgery, as well as the difficulty required to maintain large estates and pass them down to posterity. However, concerning everything connected to the accumulation of knowledge and skill, Solomon admonishes us to consider these to be good things, to have the purpose of serving our callings in life, to be taught as necessary,

[4] Eccl. 2:2.

and to pursue such domestic duties. But in this way—that we do not imagine that we will find our peace of mind in these matters. For there are countless useless ways we spend our time, and many such ways are simply misguided. But in our grief, let us not be given over to our sorrows when the outcomes that we strived or hoped for do not materialize. Instead, we must patiently suffer under the will of God and continue to do those things which are necessary.

The text itself adds this by way of conclusion: "Contentment comes from the hand of God."[5] Likewise: "To the one who pleases God, God gives wisdom and joy, but to the sinner, God gives toil."[6] In this way, it does not follow that Solomon rejects examining this teaching, but instead wishes that everyone would submit to his or her calling and find peace of mind in God—whether labors succeed or not. Indeed, we must not abandon our callings or anger God even when we experience life outcomes unequally. Nor may we abandon the pursuit of those things which are necessary even when we are not able to understand everything, just as the knowledge of all things will never uncover a way to remove death or even take away other miseries in this life. For as Solomon says here, "Both the wise and the fool die."[7] Solomon is describing those things which we perceive with our eyes; he does not want us to abandon our calling because of such outcomes. For instance, Aristotle was learned and yet he died as an exile. Indeed, they say that Aristotle died in anguish because he was not able to discover the source of the flux and reflux of the Euripus [Strait].[8]

---

[5] Eccl. 2:24.

[6] Eccl. 2:26.

[7] Eccl. 2:16.

[8] An ancient tradition, prevalent among Christians, is that Aristotle died, perhaps through drowning, because he was not able to discover the source of the tide of the Euripus, a straight lying between the Greek island of Euboea and mainland Greece. So curious was the source of this tide that a term called "the euripus phenomenon" was coined to describe uncertain currents. Coincidentally, this same tradition is probably the source of Melanchthon's belief that Aristotle died in exile on this island of Euboea, either because he drowned in the strait or because he died in heartbreak that he could not solve the riddle of the Euripus. Either way, the point that Melanchthon wishes to make—namely, that the greatest minds in the world die just like everyone else—stands strong.

To summarize this chapter, everything must be constantly referred back to the rule handed down here. That is, let us make use of those things that have been ordained, let us be subject to the governing powers, let us carry out our domestic responsibilities, let us learn those things which are necessary, and let us acknowledge the God who has ordained all such things, giving thanks to God for so many blessings, and, if something unexpected does happen, let us patiently bear it in the knowledge that it falls under God's will. In short, as has been frequently stated: "Be subject to and in prayer to God."[9]

9 Ps. 37:7 (Vulgate 36:7).

Ecclesiastes 3

[3:1-11a]

Now, expressly after these lamentations, Solomon adds in this third chapter an explicit conclusion and assertion: "God has made everything beautiful in its time."[1] That is to say, the use of things—as established by God—is good and auspicious in its own time, that is, when we use them according to God's design and in association with God's help. As it is said: "A person can only receive that which is given them from above."[2] As a result, after a long litany of thoughts, Solomon adds the following statement, "All things have their time,"[3] by which he means that it is not up to us to choose happy times without the specific calling and help of God. For instance, Brutus, Cicero, Hirtius, and Pansa[4] speculated that the old ways of the Roman Republic could be restored. However, they were wrong. And, in fact, many others have likewise been deceived and will continue to be deceived in the future. For the truth of the matter is that troubles arise when we follow our callings even with God's help—sometimes involving more difficulty and sometimes less. We see this taught in Psalms: "Commend your way to God, and he will act for you."[5]

---

[1] Eccl. 3:11.

[2] Jn. 3:27.

[3] Eccl. 3:1.

[4] These men were all Romans who served in leadership roles in the Roman Republic during the first century BCE.

[5] Ps. 37:5.

[3:11b]

"God has set the world in the human heart, yet that heart can discover neither the beginning nor the end of the work God has done."[6]

That is, God has constructed things in such a way that our hearts ought to enjoy them sweetly, praise the Designer, and relish in the peace in God. For God has given us food, pleasures, riches, the arts, different forms of governments, and virtue. However, this sweetness becomes sour to human beings as a result of their unsettled desires and tendency to follow meaningless pursuits that are spurred by human boredom, for they want nothing more than to have anything that is new and to be stimulated by that which is useless. As Jeremiah put it so pointedly and accurately: "The human heart is deceitful and desperate."[7] For example, although Marc Antony had acquired the most prosperous part of the Roman Empire, his restless nature—he wanted the whole empire—eventually summoned him to destruction because he longed for more. Similarly, Bellerophontes[8] was initially allowed to ride [the winged horse] Pegasus to perform useful tasks, however, Bellerophontes later became overly confident when he decided to ride Pegasus all the way to a meeting led by Jupiter [on Mount Olympus] and he ended up falling to the ground. To counteract these evils, people ought to stay put in their place, submit to God in faith, and do only that which is necessary. For, as Solomon says, "this is the gift of God."[9] This takes us to the next set of verses in this text.

---

[6] Eccl. 3:11.

[7] Jer. 17:9.

[8] In Greek mythology, Pegasus was an untamed winged horse and the offspring of the god Poseidon. Bellerophontes (also called Bellerophon) was a great hero akin to Heracles or Perseus. With the aid of the goddess Athena, Bellerophontes captured Pegasus, but later brazenly tried to ride Pegasus to attend a meeting of the gods on Mount Olympus. This angered Zeus, causing Bellerophontes to fall off Pegasus, as mentioned here.

[9] Eccl. 3:13.

[3:12–13]

"There is nothing better for people than to be happy and to do good while they live. Each one should eat and drink and find satisfaction in their work, for this is the gift of God."[10]

These words do not encourage us to imitate the lifestyle of a glutton. Rather, these words are an assertion of proper teaching that leads to an established conclusion, which approves the use of such things, as God has established. Solomon says that with God's help such things will bring joy and taste sweet. Solomon, therefore, commands us to use things based on how God has established them, teaching us how things are to be asked for: namely, so that they are made subject [to God] so that their use brings joy. Faith should look to God, perform the duties of our calling, ask for and expect help and success from God, and endure hardships, and inasmuch as labor brings joy, faith knows that it is aided and governed by God, and so, accordingly, it gives God thanks.

This is the meaning of the following words: that one should "find satisfaction in their work, for this is the gift of God."[11] Because God has both established work and exhorted us to do work, Solomon writes that work becomes joyful and pleasing when aided by God. Such a meaning agrees with the entirety of the psalm, "Unless the Lord builds the house, the builders labor in vain."[12] And: "Like the arrows in the hand of the powerful, so are the children of the strong."[13] This is how the kingship of Jehoshaphat went. Although he caused some scandals, he, aided by God, nonetheless mainly experienced happiness and health, and submitted himself to God.[14] By contrast, the kingship of Ahaz was restless and unpleasant because

---

[10] Eccl. 3:12–13.

[11] Eccl. 3:13.

[12] Ps. 127:1. As was typical in the Middle Ages and Renaissance, Melanchthon calls the whole psalm by its first verse.

[13] Ps. 127:4.

[14] To learn more about the kingship of Jehoshaphat, see 2 Chronicles 17–20.

Ahaz lacked faith and shirked his responsibilities in his pursuit of human wisdom.[15]

[3:14]

"All the works performed by God endure are firm..."[16]

This sentiment remains from what was spoken earlier, namely, that human plans void of God do not prosper, as we see attested, for instance, in the kingships of Ahaz and Agesilaus.[17] On the contrary, God's works are strong, that is, stable, prosperous, and enduring—which we see through David's success in battles and Jehoshaphat's stable kingship—despite the devil's constant attempts to thwart God.

But above all, the following rhetorical conclusion [*epiphonema*] rounds off our discussion: "God does these things in order to be feared."[18] This phrase about the fear of God, which has been repeated several times in this book, shows that Solomon has not presented empty arguments in some sort of philosophical manner, such as is said in the following poem: "While we speak, envious times will have escaped us. Therefore, seize the day, trusting in the future as little as possible."[19] Rather, Solomon hands down to us the most necessary rule of life, namely, that we are to place ourselves within the boundaries of our calling, condemn our own human confidence, curiosity, and other wayward desires, discern God's will, and teach Law and Gospel.[20] Consequently, God punishes Lysander, Agesilaus, Brutus,

---

[15] To learn more about the kingship of Ahaz, see 2 Kings 16 and 2 Chronicles 28.

[16] Eccl. 3:14.

[17] Ahaz was king of Judah from 732–716 BCE, while Agesilaus (II) was king of Sparta from 400–360 BCE.

[18] Eccl. 3:14.

[19] Horace, *Odes* 1.11. John Conington's nineteenth-century English translation beautifully brings out the poetry of this passage: "In the moment of our talking, envious time has ebb'd away. Seize the present; trust tomorrow e'en as little as you may," in Horace, *The Odes and Carmen Saeculare of Horace*, trans. John Conington (London: George Bell & Sons, 1882).

[20] Melanchthon literally uses the words "fear and faith," but this is shorthand for "Law and Gospel."

Antony, and countless others because they allow themselves to do things outside of their calling—whether due to undue curiosity or pure ambition. Likewise, God punishes Alexander because, after becoming so arrogant that he actually kills his friends, he wants to be worshipped as a god. God's punishment of these offenders—and, vice versa, God's offering of stability to the governments of leaders that called upon him—reminds us of the fear of God, and God teaches us by these very examples to neither rush above and beyond our callings in some sort of false confidence nor indulge ourselves in vain curiosity or evil desires. Instead, he teaches us to acknowledge our own weakness, fear God, obey God's commands, ask for and expect God's help in faith, and be subject to him.

[3:15a]

"What has happened remains."[21]

Solomon speaks here about events that come about, explaining that human deliberations not directed by God are in vain, as we see, for instance, in the life of Antony, who vainly tried to seize the monarchy, but Augustus prevailed. And, in fact, because God directed this event, it was not possible for Augustus to have been hindered by human plans. It is about such events that Solomon is speaking when he writes: "That which has already happened remains,"[22] that is, that which God leads and supports will come about, and this teaching correlates exactly with the following general rule: "Unless the Lord builds the house, the builders labor in vain."[23] Likewise: "No one is able to receive anything unless it is given to them from heaven."[24] And also: "Without me, you can do nothing."[25]

---

[21] Eccl. 3:15a.
[22] Eccl. 3:15a.
[23] Ps. 127:1.
[24] Jn. 3:27.
[25] Jn. 15:5.

[3:15b-3:16]

"Those things which will happen have already happened..."[26]

Solomon says that the things that will happen end up happening because God decreed them from long before. For instance, Cyrus was to be king and, therefore, could not have been killed by [his grandfather] Astyages, since God had decreed this event from long before.[27] This simple interpretation is the natural meaning of this text. It has often been said that many warnings are contained in this teaching. And because human endeavors without God are in vain, you must only follow God's commands and ask that God guide and help you, for God wants to help those seeking to be obedient to their calling and invoking God's name. As it is said in Psalms: "Commend your way to God, and he will act for you."[28]

[3:17a]

"God will judge both the righteous and the wicked."[29]

Here again follow examples of human miseries and catastrophes. Many things are done unjustly even in a government that is not tyrannical. That's because those who are good in the government cannot assume charge of business; on the contrary, many things are done by negligent people as well as those who are wicked that succumb to their evil desires. Meanwhile, though, God preserves the political order and judges it in its own time.

---

[26] Eccl. 3:15b.

[27] Astyages was the last king of the Median Empire. He ruled from 585 to 550 BCE before being dethroned by his grandson Cyrus in 550.

[28] Ps. 37:5.

[29] Eccl. 3:17a.

[3:17b-22]

"I said in my heart about the human race..."[30]

Here in this last section of the chapter, Solomon adds a general lament regarding the confusion of human life with external appearances. For instance, he says that it "seems" that humans and animals die alike. Interpreters have poured a lot of sweat into this passage. For instance, they said that Solomon makes this comparison in reference to what Epicureans believe. However, the truth is that Solomon is speaking about external appearances. For, certainly, if our human insight and human reason were alone consulted—without the aid of the Word of God—then it would only seem natural that human life proceeds in complete chaos and solely through chance, such that humans are like an army of ants that will be trampled. However, despite how things appear, Solomon will later explain that this is opposed to the Word of God.

30 Eccl. 3:18.

Ecclesiastes 4

[4:1-3]

**"When I turned my attention to other things,
I saw the oppression that takes place under the Sun,
and I heard the cries of the innocent..."[1]**

Here at the beginning of the fourth chapter, Solomon returns to the topic of injustices, which offers a striking example of the confusion that is rampant in human life. For if consolation had not been proposed in the Gospel, then Solomon's statement that "it would be better to have never been born"[2] would be true.

[4:4]

**"I contemplated all human labors once more,
and I found them vulnerable to envy…"[3]**

Solomon provides here another example of envy. This, too, is a great hindrance to the necessary and useful actions in life, as seen, for instance, when Scipio was the source of envy upon returning from Africa [to Rome].[4]

---

[1] Eccl. 4:1. As usual, Melanchthon cites only part of a verse but evokes an entire section (as seen in the next sentence).

[2] Eccl. 4:3.

[3] Eccl. 4:4a.

[4] Scipio (236–183 BCE) was a Roman general who received fame and glory after defeating Hannibal, thereby ending the Second Punic War. For his

[4:5-12]

"The fool folds his hands together and eats his own flesh..."[5]

Solomon adds additional examples of sloth and greed. And in his reproach of the latter, he proceeds to the topic regarding the praise of community. He reminds us that what is necessary for life is human community, offices, the arts, artisans, and orders [within society]. Indeed, all orders of society are in need of mutual support, and each person should dedicate his or her work to the common welfare of society, to the preservation of his or her own congregation, and to the vigilance needed to prevent its destruction. As it is said: "On its own, that which is good is conservative, convergent, and communicative. By contrast, that which is evil is dissipative and destructive."[6] Indeed, a greedy person only has regard for his own needs, even at the expense of a community's destruction. Solomon rebukes this kind of evil.

[4:13-17]

"It is better to be poor and wise than a king who is old and foolish..."[7]

Solomon adds here another example of ambition and unrest in government. For example, when rulers become restless in their positions of authority, they disturb too many things without necessity and, consequently, they are punished, as we see attested in the lives of Saul, Eurystheus, and countless others.[8]

---

exploits, Scipio was given the title *Africanus*, meaning something like "conqueror of Africa."

[5] Eccl. 4:5.

[6] This is possibly Pseudo-Dionysius, *On the Divine Names* 4.23.

[7] Eccl. 4:13.

[8] Saul was the first king of Israel, while Eurystheus was a mythological king in ancient Greece. Both Saul and Eurystheus met the same fate: They were ignobly defeated by their enemies and their sons died in battle with them.

Ecclesiastes 5

[5:1a]

"Keep watch over your feet when you enter the house of God, and approach for the purpose of listening."[1]

Solomon returns here to various precepts. He starts by distinguishing true worship of God from hypocritical worship, calling us back from an outward form of worship full of human confusion toward [true] knowledge of God, which leads us to reflect upon the divine commandments and promises. Accordingly, the bumblers who dreamed up that Solomon's book was secular in nature or written by an Epicurean are clearly refuted in the testimony of this chapter.

For Solomon teaches in the very beginning here that the chief end of worship is to listen to the Word of God, that is, the [divine] commandments and promises, and to obey God in true faith, as it is commanded using the same words in Jeremiah 7: "I did not make commands regarding burnt-offerings but, instead, made the following command: 'Listen to my voice, and I will be your God and you will be my people.'"[2] Here it must be understood that this whole teaching concerns the first commandment. And Solomon does not make mention of the "house of God"[3] in vain. For he admonishes us to inquire about the doctrine of the Church and true ministry with the result that we hear what the Church teaches. As it is said elsewhere: "Unless they had plowed with my heifer, they would not

---

[1] Eccl. 5:1a (or 4:17 in some versions).

[2] Jer. 7:22–23.

[3] Eccl. 5:1.

have solved my riddle."[4] Likewise in Deuteronomy 17: "You must go to the priests, for they are the ones who will teach you according to the law of God."[5] In this way, Solomon expressly unites the law and the teachers.

[5:1b]

"This is better than the sacrifice of fools."[6]

Many people dream up that ceremonies are the only way to worship God. But this is exactly how pagans worshiped God through gestures; and, as Plato [rightly] said, "Their foolishness is in plain sight."[7] For the law says, "You shall love the Lord your God with your whole heart."[8] Others, unwilling to acknowledge that ceremonies are insufficient, demand an external method of moral works like the Pharisees. But when it comes to true worship of God, there is no method that can be devised without repentance and faith. As it is said in Matthew 5: "Unless your righteousness surpasses that of the Pharisees..."[9] However, repentance and faith that receive forgiveness of sin come through [Christ] the Mediator must occur in the heart. Solomon preaches here about these distinctions by explaining above all that our hearts must be governed by the Word of God, Law, and Gospel.[10]

It has always been a common practice to heap sacrifices and invent various forms of worship and, in this way, pagans, Pharisees, and monks have departed from the voice of God. Solomon condemns such human brazenness and asserts that it is nothing but hideous

[4] Judg. 14:18.

[5] Deut. 17:9.

[6] Eccl. 5:1b (or 4:17 in some versions).

[7] Source of quote unknown.

[8] Deut. 6:5. Additionally, Jesus quotes this important verse in the Gospels (e.g., Matt. 22:37, Lk. 10:27, and Mk. 12:30).

[9] Matt. 5:20.

[10] As elsewhere, Melanchthon sometimes uses "fear and faith" (*timor et fides*) to refer to the Lutheran emphasis on "Law" and "Gospel."

sin even though humankind has the audacity to suppose that this superstition is an excellent virtue. Therefore, he adds, "They do not know how much evil they do."[11]

[5:2]

"Do not be quick to speak or utter a word..."[12]

In the section above, Solomon commanded us to listen to, learn from, and meditate on the Word of God in accordance with this saying: "Your word is a lamp to my feet."[13] And here he adds the consequence of that thought, namely, that when the Word of God is heard, the prohibition follows that you should not teach, affirm, or act contrary to the Word of God as did, for instance, the pagans, Pharisees, popes, and monks when they invented their own worship practices and rituals concerning to the Word of God. The same can be said for [Paul of] Samosata, Arius, and Absalom,[14] who all audaciously invented their own dogmas contrary to the Word of God. Similarly, [Marc] Antony[15] and many others were moved in their use of power to act contrary to the Word of God

---

[11] Eccl. 5:1/4:17.

[12] Eccl. 5:2.

[13] Ps. 119:105.

[14] Paul of Samosata was bishop of Antioch from 260 to 268 but was also known for his heretical views regarding Adoptionism, which undermined Jesus's divinity, while Arius was a priest in Alexandria (d. 336) most notoriously known for the heretical view of Arianism, which asserted that Jesus was not coequal with God the Father. Absalom was the third son of King David whose rebellion against his father (mostly recorded in 2 Samuel 13–18) ushered his ignoble death. [Possibly, Melanchthon is referring to Absalon (1128–1201), a Danish bishop and archbishop.]

[15] Marc Antony (83–30 BCE) was the Roman general who assumed control of Rome (as part of the Second Triumvirate) when Caesar was assassinated in 44. Antony eventually fell out of favor with Octavian/Augustus and remained with Cleopatra in Alexandria rather than return to Rome and come under the authority of Octavian/Augustus; he subsequently committed suicide. Perhaps this is what Melanchthon is referring to.

without any calling to do so. Moreover, Josiah, though a holy man, nevertheless stumbled in this area when he started a war that was not necessary.[16] In this way, Solomon's preaching here is a statement applicable to all people, namely, that they should listen to the Word of God and assert nothing in the Church that has not been handed down by God. Nor should governments do anything beyond their calling or beyond what is necessary. Peter says it best: "Whoever speaks should speak the oracles of God,"[17] particularly when teaching; and "whoever administers should administer by virtue of the power God supplies," namely, by remaining within the parameters of one's calling as assisted by God and not desiring to be assisted by God. God does not want to help those tempted out of curiosity away from their calling, according to what is said in Psalms: "Commend your way to God, and he will act for you."[18] In brief, Peter's words above agree exactly with this *locus* of Solomon's.

Solomon then adds a threat: "God is in heaven,"[19] meaning that God is Examiner, Judge, and Avenger. As Psalm 33 says, "God sees the whole human race…and understands all their works."[20] Likewise: "God repays everyone according to their works."[21]

---

[16] Josiah was king of Judah from 640–609 BCE and generally portrayed as a godly king in the Bible. For reasons not clear, Josiah fought against Necho II, king of Egypt, at Megiddo and was fatally wounded.

[17] 1 Pet. 4:11.

[18] Ps. 37:5.

[19] Eccl. 5:2.

[20] Ps. 33:13, 15. Of course, Melanchthon refers to this as Psalm 32 since he is using the Latin version.

[21] Rom. 2:6.

[5:3]

"Dreams follow many concerns, and foolishness comes with many words."[22]

There are different kinds of concerns.[23] For instance, there is concern for work, concern for outcomes, and concerns for going beyond one's calling. First, concern for work is strictly commanded. For instance, Romans 12 says, "The one who leads must do so with diligence."[24] Likewise in 1 Corinthians 4: "It is necessary for those in ministry to be faithful."[25] But negligence is like perfidy. In this way, David's exercising of concern must be praised, since he could anticipate the times and places that were suitable for battle. As Alexander said to Parmenion, "Do you really think I would be able to sleep before arranging for battle?"[26] However, David was in the habit of seeking from God a fortunate outcome when in battle and thereby commend this concern to God.

On the contrary, a sin against this principle is committed in two ways. The first is when a person's faulty belief in himself leads him to declare certain victory based on his strength or fortune, as seen, for instance, with Pompey.[27] The second is when a person is wracked with

---

[22] Eccl. 5:3 (5:2 in Vulgate).

[23] The Latin word *cura* is capable of many possible translations: "care," "cure," "concern," "consideration," "attention," "anxiety," "worry," "solicitude," "charge," "administration," "office," and so on. In this chapter, I have translated this word as either "care[s]" and "concern[s]," depending on context, but the other translations should be kept in mind.

[24] Rom. 12:8.

[25] 1 Cor. 4:2.

[26] Parmenion (400–330 BCE) was one of Alexander the Great's generals. This story occurred in the Greek's campaign against the Persians in 334. Parmenion advised delaying attack to allow the men to recover from exhaustion, while Alexander preferred to attack immediately. Exact source of quote unknown.

[27] Gnaeus Pompeius Magnus (106–48 BCE), better known as Pompey [the Great], was a Roman general active during the transition from the Roman Republic to the Roman Empire. Melanchthon is probably referring to the Battle of Pharsalus (also called the Battle in Thessalia) that took place in the

mistrust, as seen, for instance, with Aratus.[28] In this passage, Solomon rebukes this kind of care, which is distressed about the outcome.

There is also another reprehensible care, which has to do with unnecessarily moving a person from his or her calling. This is called "meddlesomeness,"[29] and it is frequently prohibited [in Scripture]. For instance, Paul said, "Do what is appropriate [to your calling]."[30] And from Peter we read: "Do not be like those who meddle in another's affairs."[31] These two kinds of cares are useless, and they torment our minds in vain. Consequently, it is added here: "Such cares cause many nightmares."[32] And although it is explained here that such cares produce many feelings of anxiety, I think what is meant here is that the very anxieties that have been prohibited are nothing but worthless nightmares. For example, Cassius's and Brutus's[33] meddlesomeness[34] in wanting to create a beautiful state of the Roman Republic was a

---

year 48. This is when Pompey's army greatly outnumbered Caesar's army, leading Pompey to the faulty belief that he would defeat Caesar. However, the opposite occurred. Caesar won and Pompey fled. Melanchthon is probably using Plutarch's *Parallel Lives* for these stories.

[28] Aratus of Sicyon (217–213 BCE) was a Greek general for and advisor to the Macedonian king Philip V. Melanchthon may be referring to events later in Aratus's life. After the Social War lasting from 220 to 217 BCE, Aratus lost favor with King Philip. According to Plutarch's *Parallel Lives*, vol. 11, King Philip had Aratus poisoned.

[29] The ancient Greek term πολυπραγμοσύνη can be translated in any number of ways: "capriciousness," "changeability," "officiousness," "meddlesomeness" "busybodyness," etc. Plato uses the term in *Republic* 4.434b and 444b.

[30] Phil. 1:8?

[31] 1 Pet. 4:15. The Greek word Melanchthon uses, which I translate as "those who meddle in another's affairs," is a quotation of the Greek word in 1 Pet. 4:15: ἀλλοτριεπίσκοπος. It is the only time this Greek word appears in the New Testament. Literally, it means something like "the one who oversees the affairs of another."

[32] Eccl. 5:2.

[33] Brutus and Cassius were Roman senators active in the first century BCE who had a different vision for the Roman Republic than their contemporary Julius Caesar. In fact, they were two of the most prominent leaders in the plot to assassinate Caesar, which occurred in 44 BCE. Both men were actively involved in the stabbings that led to Caesar's death.

[34] In Greek: πολυπραγμοσύνη.

completely useless dream. This Greek saying applies to the situation: "Vain people do vain things due to evil desires."[35] As a result, let this rule be your concern: "Commend your way to God, and God will do it."[36] The first part of this verse directs us to show concern for our calling and faith, while the second part adds a promise: "God will do it."

[5:2b]

"The voice of a fool is marked by loquaciousness."[37]

Solomon repeats this admonition frequently: "People should not rush to make judgments when it comes to doctrines or deliberations but, instead, should only do so after rightly considering the sources and true causes for a long time." For it is quite clear that those who are rash are often wrong and judge many things erroneously. For instance, Proverbs 10 says, "In loquaciousness, sin is not lacking."[38] And there are many similar admonitions that prohibit gossip,[39] rashness of judgment, and similar vices.

[5:3-4]

"If you make a vow to God, do not delay in fulfilling it."[40]

Solomon provides an example here of rashness of speech concerning vows. But let us also understand that many other items are

---

[35] In Greek: Μάταιοι μάταια λογίζονται διὰ ἐπιθυμίας. Melanchthon cites this same quote in his commentary on Proverbs 27 but never identifies the source.

[36] Ps. 37:5.

[37] Eccl. 5:3 (5:2b in Vulgate).

[38] Prov. 10:19.

[39] The word *garrulitas* is capable of many possible translations: "chattering," "prating," "talkativeness," "gossip," and "garrulity."

[40] Eccl. 5:5 (5:3a in Vulgate).

simultaneously included under this principle, such as oaths, contracts, pledges, and judgments about doctrine, and deliberations. For in all these items, it is necessary to avoid falling headlong [into error] or displaying rashness, and, following this verse, a very serious warning about providence is added. For example, because rashness of this sort is preoccupied only with protecting oneself, which does not care about God's judgment, it is incited either by undue admiration of one's own wisdom, or by jealousy, or by other desires. Either way, the result is the same: Rashness gets in the way of good doctrine, meaning that it moves that which should not be moved. In fact, let this admonition about providence be fixed in our minds, and let this assent be confirmed in us by the examples of all the punishments that we read about and see on a daily basis. For the divine voice that Solomon preaches about here regarding providence is set against rashness, of which we see the examples of punishments, reliance upon foolishness, human doubt, and all the [false] opinions of the Epicureans and the uncivilized.

[5:5-6]

"...in the presence of an angel..."[41]

It was customary for the [biblical] patriarchs and prophets to call God's Son "the angel" because they knew that this Lord, who had been promised to the Church, would be a marvelous messenger of the decree regarding the liberation of the human race. In this way, Jacob called him "the angel" and added a description that distinguished him from created angels. Jacob said, "May the angel who delivered me from all harm bless you."[42] He therefore affirmed that this angel was almighty, liberating from sin and death, and makes mention of him, knowing that, properly speaking, he is the Lord and Guardian of the Church.

---

[41] Eccl. 5:6 (5:5 in Vulgate). In Latin, the word *angelus* can also mean "messenger," particularly when translating the Greek cognate ἄγγελος.

[42] Gen. 48:16.

[5:8]

"If you see the oppression of the poor and violation of judgments..."

Solomon then adds a warning lest there should be any doubt of providence given that so many wrongs are permitted. For instance, as Diogenes once said, the man Harpalus offered a living testimony against the gods given that he lived in great pleasures even after committing many crimes.[43] However, the answer to this objection arises from experience itself. For although wrongs are permitted for a time, punishments will eventually follow. God preserves this principle, which is the fiber[44] of all discipline. For all severe offenses are punished with severe punishments in this life [in addition to the one to come]. As the saying goes: "All who draw the sword will die by the sword."[45] Likewise: "Woe to those who rob others, for you will be robbed."[46] As a result, Solomon immediately adds a threat here, saying that other, additional judges remain, by whom those who have committed unjust acts are to be punished, as Augustus punished Antonius.[47] And the famous description of the king is to be observed here which says: "There is a king who reigns above all in the land for the cultivation of the fields."[48] In this instance, Solomon

---

[43] Diogenes, also known as Diogenes the Cynic, was a Greek philosopher who died in 323 BCE. The quote comes from Cicero's *On the Nature of the Gods* 3.34. There is debate about the exact identity of the man Harpalus, but the principle behind his unjust actions stands true, namely, that he was wicked but nonetheless did not seem to experience any consequent punishment.

[44] The Latin word *nervus* can be translated in multiple ways: "tendon," "sinew," "muscle," "nerve," "string," "fiber," "power," "fetter," "strength," etc. It derives directly from the Greek word νεῦρον, which also has a range of possible meanings.

[45] Matt. 26:52.

[46] Isaiah 33:1.

[47] The Antonius mentioned here is Iullus Antonius, who lived from 43 to 2 BCE. A son of Marc Antony, he was a secret lover of Augustus's daughter Julia, who was married to another man. When this affair was revealed in 2 BCE, Augustus charged Antonius with treason and sentenced him to death.

[48] This is possibly a reference to or quote from Eccl. 5:9.

distinguishes the king from the tyrant. For while the tyrant brings ruin and devastation, the good prince fosters society and preserves the cultivation of the land, the Church, the arts, and all good things.

[5:10]

**"A greedy person will not be satisfied with money,
and the one who loves riches
will reap no reward from them."**

This section contains long sermons condemning greed.[49] For instance, Solomon repeats the concept that he mentioned earlier which commands things to be done according to the ordinances of God as they relate to food, drink, and marriage. Moreover, we are to live out our vocation in a good conscience and faith, commending to God those things over which we do not have power to change. For Solomon often reminds us how often we must bring to mind the following saying: "Commend your way to God, and he will act for you."[50]

---

[49] The word *avaritia* (and related words) can be accurately translated in many ways: "greed," "covetousness," "stinginess," "rapacity," or "avarice." I am going with "greed."

[50] Ps. 37:5.

Ecclesiastes 6

[6:1-11]

"Even a famous person is still human and cannot compete with someone who is stronger."[1]

At the end of the sixth chapter, Solomon offers a principle that guides us to perform the duties of our vocation without shrinking back from them even when we experience an outcome that is different than anticipated. For as he says, "Even a famous person is still human and cannot compete with someone who is stronger."[2] What he means is that we cannot control events, and so it follows that "words are vain,"[3] which means that our cares and concerns are in vain and of no profit to us. Our Latin text says, "what is necessary for a person is to seek greater things,"[4] but the Hebrew text says only, "they are of no profit to us." Indeed, as I said earlier, these verses admonish us to consider [only] those cares that concern us. But as for those cares that do not concern us, as we explored in three steps, we are to take care only of the labor of our vocation since our vocation does pertain to us, although the exact outcome does not. The same principle applies to other things outside of our vocation, namely, they do not pertain to us.

---

1 Eccl. 6:10.
2 Eccl. 6:10.
3 Eccl. 6:11.
4 Eccl. 7:1 in Latin Vulgate.

Ecclesiastes 7

[6:12]

"One does not know what will be of use to him or her in this life, for all our days are in vain…"[1]

Solomon continues speaking, however, about "things under the Sun,"[2] by which he means both good and bad events that occur in this mortal life. For instance, although Joseph initially thought that his being sold into slavery was detrimental, it was actually beneficial.[3] Therefore, it follows that "One cannot know what will happen under the Sun,"[4] that is to say, we cannot know what will occur [in the future]—whether we encounter prosperity or adversity. For example, David was restored after committing the greatest harm in his nation, while Saul was brought to ruin after achieving the greatest honor.[5] Consequently, Solomon orders us to be obedient to God, whether in prosperous or adverse circumstances, commending to God the outcome. When encountering prosperity, in other words, we must not tempt [God] by relying upon our own confidence or doing unjust or unnecessary things nor to fall apart in adversity or abandon God. On the contrary, we are to be

---

1 Eccl. 6:12. Although the Greek and Latin versions include this as the first verse in the seventh chapter, it appears as the last verse in chapter six in modern Bibles.

2 Eccl. 6:12b.

3 This story is told in Gen. 37:12–36.

4 Eccl. 6:12b.

5 Saul's lowest points as king are told in 1 Sam. 15, 28, and 31, while David's are told in 2 Sam. 11 and 12.

mindful of the principle taught by Job: "Though God slay me, yet I will hope in him."[6]

[7:1a]

"A good name is better than a fine perfume."[7]

Solomon brings together several observations here, some of which are designed to exhort us to action, some to be patient, some to console the poor, and some to lift up the oppressed. In every instance, though, I will highlight the details in which they are to be referred. First, what relates to a good name or honor[8] is an exhortation to action. Indeed, it has been said elsewhere what, properly speaking, qualifies as honor or a good name according to human judgment. For it is the approval of our conscience in judging rightly and [the consciences] of others who judge rightly. For example, when Scipio liberated another man's fiancée, he was shown to have [much] honor since he acted within his conscience and gained the approval of others who judged him rightly.[9] By contrast, Thraso had no honor since he himself neither judged rightly—and, instead, arrogated to himself false things—nor did others who lied by giving their approval.[10] However, God commands both that we do right things and that we approve things done rightly. As the saying goes: "You shall not give false testimony."[11]

---

[6] Job 13:15.

[7] Eccl. 7:1.

[8] The Latin word *gloria* can be accurately rendered in many ways in English: "honor," "reputation," and "glory." And in its usage in this section, I will use each of these three translations. But behind every instance is the same Latin word: *gloria*.

[9] This refers to a famous story in which Scipio (236–183 BCE), a notable Roman general and statesman, was given a beautiful woman who was captured by his troops when he was fighting in Spain. But instead of taking her, he gave her back to the man to whom she was betrothed and gave ample gifts for their marriage. This story is recorded in Livy, *The History of Rome* 26.50.

[10] It is unclear, but this Thraso appears to be a Greek ruler in modern-day India who reigned in the first century BCE.

[11] Ex. 20:16.

Indeed, God wants the knowledge of virtues to exist, both so that we acknowledge the very kind [of thing] it is and that each virtue may be the ruler of life. And in order for a distinction to be made apparent between virtues and vices, God also wills for crimes to be punished through human judgment. God rightly wills for such things to be commended for two reasons: (1) that the distinction between virtues and vices may be made more apparent and (2) that others may be instructed by such examples. In this way, God wants those who are famous to be cast out of society, but the honest person is given a place in the society with those whose morals are without reproach.

Since, therefore, such an approval has been divinely sanctioned—and is a good thing—it is evident that this honor is to be sought and, in fact, that it is a command from God that we avoid scandals. As Paul said, "Do everything for God's glory, and do not cause anyone to stumble in the Church."[12] What's more, Augustus said it well: "I need a good conscience for God's sake and a good reputation for my neighbor's."[13] And Solomon says elsewhere [in Proverbs], "A good name is better than great riches."[14] There he teaches by making distinctions [among human matters] that a good reputation[15] comes before knowledge[16] and resources. For a person is sooner to lose knowledge before reputation. And here is an even sweeter admonition: "A good reputation is better than balm,"[17] which means as follows: Just as balm heals and refreshes our bodies, so a good reputation offers great relief to our hearts. And the exact opposite equally applies: A bad reputation is a terrible butchery.[18] Therefore, it is said in Proverbs: "A good reputation strengthens the

---

[12] 1 Cor. 10:31–32.

[13] Augustine, *Sermon* 355.1.

[14] Prov. 22:1.

[15] The Latin word translated as "reputation" is *fama*, which can also mean: "fame," "rumor," or "report." It is also likely a synonym here with the Latin word *gloria*, "honor," "reputation," or "glory."

[16] The Latin word translated as "knowledge" is *facultatibus*, which can also mean: "resources," "skills," "opportunities," or "abilities."

[17] Exact citation unknown.

[18] It is not clear if Melanchthon is quoting a saying or just making a deduction.

bones."[19] Likewise, Pindarus said, "Like warm water that refreshes our wearied bones, so is honor."[20] Similarly, Thucydides wrote, "Honor is like food to the elderly."[21] Such things must be properly understood and distinguished from the boasting of our conscience, the approval of others, and the boasting of righteousness before God. As it is said elsewhere, "Let the one who boasts boast in the Lord."[22]

And, in another place, there is something spoken about the approval of our conscience: "This is our boast: the testimony of our conscience."[23] Likewise: "Let every person test his own work, and then the reason for his boasting will be in himself alone and not in others."[24] What Paul means in this verse is that each is to examine one's own deeds, and if done correctly, you will have the approval of your conscience, which is the honor about which we have been speaking. We must not do what so many do, namely, increase the criticism of others or seek the approval of the masses.

[7:1b]

"The day of our death is better than the day of our birth."[25]

This saying offers consolation. For Solomon makes a comparison not simply between life and death but between adversity and deliverance. But this must be acknowledged by faith. And in the Church, this saying about the fate of believers is neither obscure nor ambiguous. On the contrary, it aligns with a similar saying found in Revelation 14: "Blessed are the dead who die in the Lord."[26] For

19 Prov. 15:30.

20 Exact citation unknown.

21 Exact citation unknown, probably either Thucydides' *History of the Peloponnesian War* or Pericles' *Funeral Oration*.

22 1 Cor. 1:31.

23 2 Cor. 1:12.

24 Gal. 6:4.

25 Eccl. 7:1b.

26 Rev. 14:13.

such sayings offer a testimony about the life to come. As Proverbs 14 says: "The righteous retain hope even in their death."[27] Likewise in Job: "Though God slay me, yet I will hope in him."[28] I will not seek out different interpretations of this passage or add something from pagan writers such as: "It is best not to be born, or [the next best is] to die as soon as possible."[29] For such convictions lie outside the doctrine of the Church.

[7:2-6]

"It is better to go to a house of mourning than a house of feasting..."[30]

These sayings[31] align with several well-known thoughts. For instance: "Feelings run wild in prosperity."[32] Likewise: "The people sat down to eat and got up to play."[33] Also: "It is good that you humbled me because it taught me your statutes."[34] Similarly: "Hardship offers understanding."[35] During times of prosperity, people become more [spiritually] negligent, thinking about God's wrath less and seeking out God's help less. They then become even more insolent, relying on their own energy and power, and leaving them easy targets for the devil. And from that mountaintop, they subsequently fall headlong into great calamities. As the saying goes: "The unjust are raised

---

27 Prov. 14:32b.

28 Job 13:15.

29 Sophocles, *Oedipus Rex* 1225. In Greek: τὸ δ', ἐπεὶ φανῇ, βῆναι κεῖθεν ὅθεν περ ἥκει, πολὺ δεύτερον, ὡς τάχιστα. All translations are my own.

30 Eccl. 7:2.

31 We must always keep in mind that Melanchthon thinks in *loci*, not individual verses. And here, he is referring to this and several of the following verses.

32 Ovid, *Art of Love* 2.437. Ovid, who lived a generation before Jesus, was one of the most famous Roman poets. His *Art of Love* was amusing, provocative, and elegant.

33 Ex. 32:6 and 1 Cor. 10:7

34 Ps. 119:71 (118:71 in Vulgate).

35 Isa 28:19.

up so that they may be hurled down."[36] By contrast, hardships are reminders of our weakness and our need to seek God's help, and they also provide the curbing of many desires. Consequently, the Church is subject to the cross, as has often been said elsewhere about the causes of the Church's misfortunes and about its true consolation.

What Solomon expresses at the end of these sayings [7:2–6] is that the joy of fools will by no means last forever and, instead, that fools will fall swiftly from their false sense of security and insolence into tragic calamities. For instance, we see this in the lives of Saul, David, Croesus, Xerxes, Alexander [the Great], Pompey, Caesar, [Marc] Antony, and countless others who were overcome by the most unfortunate of circumstances to the degree that they may be seen as examples of God's wrath as a way to prompt the rest of us to repent, fear God, and pray. For God will preserve the following rule: "Whatever is lofty in the eyes of people is an abomination in the eyes of God."[37] Likewise: "God has scattered the proud in the conceit of their heart."[38] And consequently, Solomon compares the brevity of the joy of fools to the sound of thorns burning quickly.[39]

---

[36] Claudius Claudianus, otherwise known as Claudian, was a Greek-speaking poet who wrote in Latin and who lived from c. 370 to 404 CE. This excerpt comes from a passage in his book *Against Rufinus* 1.21–23. Rufinus was a Byzantine minister opposed by Claudian, who probably wrote the poem against Rufinus in the year 396.

[37] This is possibly a quote from Prov. 16:5.

[38] Lk. 1:51.

[39] This is a reference to Eccl. 7:6.

[7:7]

"Deceit[40] troubles the wise and destroys their noble heart."[41]

As is evident throughout history, deceit is detestable. Indeed, in every act of governance, deceit is a highly infectious plague, and countless leaders such as Palamedes, Miltiades, Aristides, Cimon, and Themistocles were oppressed by deceitful actions. Regrettably, examples of this evil are neither rare not obscure. And their sources are well known. By nature, after all, people are proud. Their pride only varies in degree. Therefore, people envy others' honor and seek to diminish it through a web of deception that invalidates the honorable person's counsel and deeds. This attempt at sophistic invalidation is called deceit.[42] Though pernicious anywhere, it is much more pernicious in the Church, where sophistries and tricks are perpetrated to foil the simple truth and invalidate those things that have been rightly taught. Now, on this matter, it has been divinely commanded in the Second Commandment[43] lest the truth contained in the [Church's] teaching be corrupted. And concerning other matters, we are told: "You shall not give false witness."[44] These commandments remind us to detest and flee from sophistries and deception.

---

[40] The Latin word *calumnia* can be translated in various ways: "deceit," "trickery," "lying," "pretense," "false accusation," "slander," "extortion," "bribery," "trouble," "evasion," and "calumny."

[41] Eccl. 7:7. The Latin version differs slightly from more modern versions.

[42] Once again, the Latin word used is *calumnia*.

[43] In the Lutheran tradition, following the Greek and Latin Vulgate rather than the Hebrew, the Second Commandment is: "You shall not take the name of the Lord your God in vain."

[44] In the Lutheran tradition, this is the Eighth Commandment.

[7:8a]

"The end of an undertaking is better than its beginning."[45]

In general, Solomon suggests that the end of an undertaking should be the result of careful planning, as if to say that it is better to foresee a plan's goal than its beginning. As the saying goes: "Whatever you do, do it wisely and keep the end in view."[46] Or, alternatively, the simple explanation is that we understand Solomon's saying as referring to good and honorable counsel. When understood accordingly, the end of an undertaking is perceived as better in two ways: first, in the perseverance of the will to accomplish an honorable thing and, then, in its success. For instance, many reckless people[47] are courageous in the beginning of an undertaking—whether it is in learning, in going to war, or in causing an uproar. But when the going gets tough and they experience a setback, they reject their confession [of faith in teaching], desert the field of battle, and the like. As a result, Solomon indicates in this saying that perseverance should be the hallmark of good counsel. As it is said in the Gospel: "Whoever perseveres to the end will be saved."[48] Besides this, an honorable cause is better than its success, for although it may suffer many setbacks, an honorable cause will [ultimately] prevail in the end.

---

[45] Eccl. 7:8a.

[46] This Latin quote appears to have originated in the Middle Ages. It has been inaccurately attributed to classical writers such as Ovid. It can be found in various sources, e.g., *Gesta Romanorum* (Köln: Ulrich Zell, 1472), 162 [81 verso].

[47] Melanchthon uses the Greek word θρασύδειλοι, which generally refers to those who are reckless, bold, daring, or insolent.

[48] Matt. 24:13.

[7:8b-9]

"Patience is better than arrogance."[49]

Pride is the source of impatience, and it is also the source of desire for revenge and strife. As it is said in Proverbs: "Contention resides among the proud."[50] Consequently, great dissensions have arisen in both empires and in the Church. For instance, because Alcibiades and Coriolanus could not bear injury with patience, they went to war against their own people.[51] By contrast, Camillus, Fabius, and Scipio were able to endure injury.[52] Indeed, the verse is well known that says: "He did not put rumors ahead of safety."[53] And it is also said about this forbearance and restraint: "Blessed are the meek, for they will inherit the earth."[54] Likewise in Proverbs 16: "A patient person is better than one who conquers cities."[55] Therefore, the following verse in Ecclesiastes says, "Do not be quickly provoked to anger, for anger rests [only] in the breast of a fool."[56] And as such, there have

---

[49] Eccl. 7:8b.

[50] Prov. 13:10.

[51] Alcibiades and Coriolanus were both generals who lived in the fifth century BCE. Alcibiades was an Athenian whose life was marked by several defections, betrayals, and reinstatements. For instance, he defected to the Spartans, then to the Persians, and then later back to the Athenians. Gaius Marcius Coriolanus was exiled from Rome and subsequently defected to the Volsci, who were an Italian people active during the time of the Roman Republic at war with the Romans at this time.

[52] These three men were all illustrious Roman generals who stayed loyal to Rome during the Roman Republic. Marcus Furius Camillus lived in the fifth and fourth centuries BCE, Quintus Fabius Maximus Verrucosus in the third century BCE, and Publius Cornelius Scipio Africanus in the second and first centuries BCE.

[53] Cicero, *On Duties* 1.24. Cicero is quoting Quintus Ennius, of whose works only fragments remain. The "he" in this reference is Quintus Fabius Maximus Verrucosus. This saying could also be translated as: "He did not put hearsay ahead of his greetings."

[54] Matt. 5:5.

[55] Prov. 16:32.

[56] Eccl. 7:9.

been countless warnings given in all [ancient] writings about the need to control anger.

[7:10]

"Do not say, 'Why were former times better than today?'"[57]

This admonition also preaches patience. For Thucydides said about nations, "Every age is hard."[58] Indeed, living in the present is always more challenging since challenges are felt more closely in the moment. Therefore, we both praise the former times in which others lived and flee the present circumstances in which we find ourselves. Yet this rule is to be followed: "Humble yourselves under the mighty hand of God,"[59] in which is meant that we must not murmur against God and, instead, we must patiently offer obedience as we bear those burdens God imposes on the human race in every place and in every time. As Job says, "The Lord gave, and the Lord has taken away. Blessed be the name of the Lord."[60] All times, in other words, have their own challenges. For instance, although David's reign was more prosperous than Hezekiah's, both had their fair share of catastrophes. And Hezekiah was compelled to endure the evils of his own age. For it is a sign of wisdom to both bear adversity in the right manner and not extend it due to foolishness. As the saying goes: "Do not heal evil with evil."[61] Here the oft-repeated rule pertains: "May you be subject to God and pray to him."[62] Likewise, let us keep this verse from Pythagoras in mind: "Whatever your destiny, bear it in patience and do not grieve it."[63]

---

[57] Eccl. 7:10.

[58] Thucydides, source unknown. The Greek original is ἀεί τό παρόν βαρύ.

[59] 1 Pet. 5:6.

[60] Job 1:21.

[61] This is likely a reference to 1 Pet. 3:9 or Rom. 12:21. In Greek: μὴ τὸ κακόν ἰῶ κακῷ.

[62] Exact source unknown.

[63] Pythagoras. *Golden Verses* 18. In Greek: ὧν ἂν μοῖραν ἔχῃς ταύτην φέρε μήδ' ἀγανάκτει.

[7:11–14]

"Like an inheritance, wisdom is good, and it is better than seeing the Sun; that is, better than life itself. Both wisdom and riches offer protection. But the teaching of wisdom is something better because it gives life."[64]

Solomon lays the objection to rest. Previously, he said that wisdom is an affliction, for humans often stumble and often fail to respond to circumstances with good counsel. In this way, Solomon appears to want to deter people from caring for learning and governing. On the contrary, he says, I order you to learn, govern the church, common public, the management of the home, and pursue vocational training. For both these labors and the things themselves—for instance, peace and [vocational] training—are good things but their results must be commended to God. Therefore, Solomon immediately adds, "Consider the works of God, for no one can make straight what God has made crooked."[65] That is to say, human diligence can neither avoid nor cure all evils, nor should governing be rejected on that account; instead, there is to be obedience to God in our callings, clinging to this most delightful consolation. As Paul has declared, "Your work in the Lord is not in vain."[66]

As such, our minds are not to murmur against God when facing adversities. The same consolation can be found in the following: "Enjoy all the good things on a good day,"[67] which is to say, when the results are in your favor, give thanks to God and take advantage of them. However, neither assume you are entitled to prosperous things nor, being puffed up with foolish confidence, seek to impress others; indeed, do not attempt to move that which cannot be moved, as Xerxes, Pompey, and many others attempted to achieve. Instead, be humble and prepare yourself for the endurance of adversities because hard times will soon follow.

---

64 Eccl. 7:11–12.

65 Eccl. 7:13.

66 1 Cor. 15:58.

67 Eccl. 7:14.

Solomon then gives consolations in adverse times because, otherwise, people would abandon God and pursue something else. People would seek out things that are not profitable for them due to an undue curiosity, just like Bellerophon, after being puffed up with favorable circumstances, wanted to be carried by Pegasus into heaven.[68] Instead, we are to be humble, remain within the limits of our calling, and be restrained by fear of punishment lest insolence, injustice, and neglect of duty follow—and the like.

Solomon also offers consolations when facing adversities lest people abandon God and pursue something else or lest they seek refuge in devices that are not profitable, as, for example, when Saul consulted a witch and the emperors of Constantinople turned to the Turks. Instead, let us ask and wait for help from God to use the remedies ordained by him. Nor is it a secret that people greatly sin in many ways when they try to correct adversity through unprofitable remedies.

[7:15]

"The righteous perish in their righteousness while the ungodly live a long time in their ungodliness."[69]

These are two rules which, though seeming to differ, are nonetheless true and do not differ, since each scenario is decreed by God. The first is completely confined to the political order: Severe offenses are punished with severe punishments in this life. As the saying goes: "Everyone who takes up the sword will die by the sword."[70] These things regularly occur throughout the human race—whether a person's fall [from grace] remains in ungodliness or whether he

[68] In Greek mythology, Pegasus was an untamed winged horse and the offspring of the god Poseidon; Bellerophontes (also called Bellerophon) was a great hero akin to Heracles or Perseus. With the aid of the goddess Athena, he captured Pegasus but later died by falling off the creature when riding to Mount Olympus, as alluded to here.

[69] Eccl. 7:15.

[70] Matt. 26:52.

or she is converted to God, even if the punishments are mitigated after turning to God. And although no one is without fault, yet those who have not been polluted by severe offenses do not fall victim to such tragedies as shown, for instance, in the fact that Augustus died in peace.

The second rule is confined to the ecclesiastical order, namely, that the Church is subject to the cross. And as a result, Abel, Jeremiah, John the Baptist, the apostles, the martyrs, and others have been put to death. Such things do not pertain to political judgment. For instance, the Church knows that there is one set of reasons for Abel's death, and there is another set for Absalom's death.[71] But those not subject to the Church's teaching are troubled by such examples with the result that they have their doubts about providence. Nevertheless, let us understand the clear witness here of providence in that both the deaths of Abel and Absalom are typical and ordinary examples of homicide. But then, concerning the saints, we have an even clearer witness in God's presence in which Paul earlier stated that God would restore the dead to life. For instance, even though Paul was under God's care, he was nonetheless killed by Nero.

[7:16]

"Neither be overly righteous nor overly wise lest you enter into ruin."[72]

There is no doubt that Solomon is speaking here about political justice and the governance of this external life, and, as such, the meaning of this passage becomes clear and serves as a very useful command. For justice finds itself located between negligence, on the one hand, and cruelty, on the other. For example, excessive severity leads to cruelty, as was the case with Aurelianus; while excessive indulgence that does not punish severe offenses also makes one

[71] Perhaps Melanchthon is assuming that Abel's death is ecclesiastical in orientation—thus subject to the cross—while Absalom's is political in orientation.

[72] Eccl. 7:16.

wicked, as was the case with Arcadius.[73] Meanwhile, solid governance, which steers a middle course like Augustus did, follows the best route of all. As such, Solomon's admonition here is for us to seek out the medium between these two [extremes of negligence and cruelty] so that goodness will prevail. Nor is the most obscure medium to be sought out, for, in God, mercy surpasses judgment. Still, Solomon's warning must also be diligently observed when he adds: "...lest you enter into ruin." For excessive severity leads to cruelty, many sound individuals are killed for no reason, and many good people flee from governing.

But right after his admonition about not being overly righteous, Solomon immediately gives a similar one about wisdom: "Neither be overly wise..." For just as cruelty can lead to excessive severity, so excessive wisdom, that is, excessive subtlety, can lead to scorn, quarrelsomeness, meddlesomeness, sophistry, and antagonism.[74] As Menander said, "Laws are good, but anyone who interprets them too subtly becomes a sycophant."[75] For instance, it would be like someone who agreed to a thirty-day truce, only to ravage the lands at night when everyone is sleeping. Or, it would be like saying the emperor is lord of Milan while the French happens upon the subtlety in which he says that Milan belongs to him. Life is replete with such examples, and it is evident from it that wars and devastations arise from it. As a result, there are many warnings about avoiding this kind of satirical wisdom. As Agesilaus said, "A righteous cause is a very good pretext."[76]

---

[73] Aurelianus was a powerful politician and prefect who lived from 393 to 416. Arcadius was a Roman emperor who lived from 377 to 408. According to a contemporary bishop and historian, Synesius, who was personally acquainted with both men, Aurelianus was severe while Arcadius was weak.

[74] As is common, Melanchthon uses some of the ancient Greek terms rather than solely Latin ones, e.g., πολυπραγμοσύνη, "meddlesomeness," and ἀντιλογική, "antagonism." It is important to note that all these terms can be translated in more than one way.

[75] Exact location of Menander's quote unknown.

[76] Exact location of Agesilaus's quote unknown.

[7:17]

"Be neither overly wicked nor overly foolish lest you die before your time."[77]

This admonition is consistent with the following verse, which speaks about another extreme, namely, negligence. For instance, the magistrate is not to tolerate atrocious and excessive crimes; the faithful teacher must not keep silent when it comes both to necessary things and idolatry, and no one should "strain out a gnat only to swallow a camel."[78] In fact, Solomon threatens a horrible punishment upon the one who is negligent, "...lest you die before your time." What this means is that if you are negligent in upholding of your moral values and unfasten the bridle that keeps your evil desires in check, God may punish you by means of the magistrate or by some other means—for instance, in a similar way that David himself fell into punishment as a result of indulging in excessive behavior. But when he wishes the middle ground to be sought, he later adds, "Who is the one who discerns the middle ground with God showing the way and ruling one's counsel and hand? The one who fears God." Thus, Solomon cautions us stating that there is no prosperous government without fear of God, prayer, and an appeal for divine aid. As these sayings illustrate: "Unless the Lords builds the house, the laborers build in vain..."[79] And: "Commend your way to the Lord; trust in him and he will do this."[80]

---

[77] Eccl. 7:17.
[78] Matt. 23:24.
[79] Ps. 127:1 (Vulgate 126:1).
[80] Ps. 37:5 (Vulgate 36:5).

[7:18]

"It is good that you should take hold up in this; do not withdraw your hand in that. The one who fears God flees from all these things."[81]

When severity is good, exercise it, but when gentleness is beneficial, use it instead. In this passage, Solomon directs us to pursue the middle ground in accordance with each particular matter or circumstance, meaning that we sometimes act harsher and sometimes milder, just as a doctor prescribes different kinds of medicine to different patients. For instance, Fabius determined that it was sometimes right to fight and sometimes right not to fight.[82] Likewise, although Saul killed the Gibeonites in foolish zeal, Joshua spared them.[83]

In short, it is necessary to observe the rhetorical emphasis in the word "understand," because this word signifies the true reason for seeking after something—whether in severity or in gentleness. As Paul states, "Let everyone be convinced in his own mind."[84] In this way, when Solomon says that "it is good that you understand," he is referring to when the conscience has found the true matter under deliberation and is in firm agreement with it. That is because this reason should be preferred above impulsiveness and other such emotions. Now, if anyone were to ask, *How do we go about finding the middle ground or virtue that is to be applied in this circumstance?*, here is Solomon's response: "The one who fears God flees from all these things."[85] In other words, this person will select a better path because the one who fears God contemplates the divine law and, at the same time, is led by the Holy Spirit and prays to be guided in his plans through prayer, moderates his emotions, wants to look after

81 Eccl. 7:18.

82 This is most likely a reference to Quintus Fabius Maximus Verrucosus, a Roman general in the third century BCE who earned the epithet *Cunctator*, "The Delayer," due to his passive and indirect military strategy against Hannibal in the Second Punic War.

83 2 Sam. 21:1–14 and Josh. 9:1–27, respectively.

84 Rom. 14:5.

85 Eccl. 7:18b.

the interests and welfare of both the Church and state, and does not regulate his behavior out of private anger or hidden desires.

[7:19]

"Wisdom strengthens the wise more than ten princes in a city."[86]

This is a general admonition which signifies that good planning and moderation come before strength. In other words, a leader is better protected through diligence in the avoidance of dangers, with moderation in controlling one's emotions, and with prayer to God than being surrounded by great garrisons or a great army. After all, even though he seemingly slept in safety at night under the protection of the garrisons in a tower, which could only be ascended by stairs, Alexander of Pherae was nonetheless killed by his wife and her brothers.[87] Similarly, Alexander the Great's father was killed during a public parade in plain sight of the princes and his bodyguards.[88] Also, Julius [Caesar] was killed in the Senate.[89] In short, there are countless examples of this phenomenon. By contrast, other princes enjoyed a calmer and more peaceful government as well as a more tranquil death, for instance, Jehoshaphat, Augustus, and Theodosius.[90]

---

[86] Eccl. 7:19.

[87] Alexander of Pherae was a Greek ruler in the fourth century BCE. His death was described by Plutarch in his book *Parallel Lives* in the section of the "Life of Pelopidas" 35.3–7.

[88] Philip II of Macedon, Alexander the Great's father, was killed in 336 BCE by an assassin as he attended a wedding ceremony. Even though his bodyguards were close by, they had let down their guard since the occasion at hand was supposed to be a celebration.

[89] Julius Caesar was famously killed by a handful of senators in Rome on the ides of March in 44 BCE. Being in Rome on routine business among colleagues, Caesar had no reason to think he should walk with bodyguards. There are multiple ancient sources discussing Caesar's life and death.

[90] These references most likely refer to the biblical king Jehoshaphat (9th century BCE) as well as the Roman emperors Augustus (63 BCE–14 AD) and Theodosius (347–395).

[7:20]

"There is no one who is righteous on earth who always does good and does not sin."[91]

This is a political statement[92] that is not addressing the sin inherent in [human] nature but instead external errors and faults. For even the righteous and those worthy of praise err on occasion, not always in the same activity but in different ones. For example, [King] David was a good and sound ruler who usually acted righteously, nevertheless, he was negligent in many areas, including when he acted destructively as he seized the wife of a friend and then had him killed—despite the fact that the man he did this to was holy and courageous.[93] Similarly, although [King] Josiah was also a good and sound ruler, he was nevertheless motivated to provoke a war that was unnecessary.[94] In this way, not even the righteous are without their faults. Regarding this phenomenon, a verse from Theognis may be applied: "Even a virtuous person is sometimes bad and sometimes good."[95] Likewise, in Euripides we read: "The one who does many things also errs in many ways."[96]

---

[91] Eccl. 7:20.

[92] In the preface to his commentary on Proverbs, Melanchthon classifies biblical statements into various categories: theological, political, ethical, and domestic [or filial]. Theological matters are dealt with in the first table of the law [that is, of the Ten Commandments], while the other three all relate to the second table. Briefly, theological sayings refer to those touching on love for God, political to those things addressing the duties of government leaders, ethical to all people regarding instructions about how to act, and domestic [or filial] to issues surrounding marriage and management of the household.

[93] Melanchthon is referring to when David seized and had sex with Bathsheba and then killed her husband Uriah. This story is told in 2 Sam. 11.

[94] Melanchthon most likely refers to Josiah's decision to go to war with the king of Egypt in 2 Kings 23:28–29.

[95] Theognis of Megara was a Greek poet active in the sixth century BCE. Here is the quote in Greek: αὐτάρ ἀνήρ ἀγαθός πότε μέν κακός ἄλλοτε ἐσθλός. The passage is quoted in Plato, *Protagoras* 344a.

[96] Melanchthon cites Euripides as the author of this quote. Here it is in Greek: ὁ πολλά πράττων πολλά καί αμαρτάνει. The exact location is unknown.

As a result, we see here these descriptions about good and bad rulers. For example, a good ruler is one who seeks to do what is right; although he usually succeeds, he does occasionally fall short. Examples of such good rulers include David, Josiah, and [Caesar] Augustus. By contrast, a bad ruler is one who does not seek to do what is right and usually does wrong, although he does occasionally do what is right. An example of such a bad ruler includes Cambyses.[97] In this way, the distinction between the two is formed in our constant will or purpose. And such is the end goal that Paul established when he wrote that "what is required is that we would be faithful."[98] When it comes to these admonitions, let us recognize our great weakness, let us have a healthy fear of the devil's tricks, and let us constantly pray that God would rule over us and bring healing to our erring ways. As Peter commands, "Keep watch, for your adversary seeks to surround you."[99]

[7:21-22]

"Do not accommodate your heart to every word that is spoken."[100]

This admonition has to do with slander. It seeks to caution us against either becoming slanderers ourselves or becoming the object of slander or false accusations. For slander is contrary to both truth and honesty since it distorts pardonable offenses or slight mistakes and propagates a false opinion about those who are trying to do what is right. This can actually lead to people delighting in slander, similar to what Pindar wrote: "Cursed talk is like food."[101] This vice, however, is

---

[97] Melanchthon is no doubt referring to Cambyses, the Persian ruler active in the fifth century BCE, who is possibly the same person referred to by Xerxes (or Ahasuerus), as mentioned in the Bible.

[98] 1 Cor. 4:2.

[99] 1 Pet. 5:8.

[100] Eccl. 7:21.

[101] Because Melanchthon quotes Pindar—a Greek poet active in the sixth and fifth centuries BCE—in Latin paraphrase rather than the original Greek, the exact location of this quote is unknown.

prohibited in the Eight Commandment: “Do not bear false witness.”[102] Similarly, in Leviticus we read: “Do not be a whisperer among the people.”[103] Such was stated above with reference to the judgment of conscience and to reputation. Although we should attend to both, attention should first be directed to conscience lest it become diminished. Afterwards, a good reputation follows. As Augustine says: “I must have a good conscience before God and a good reputation before my neighbor.”[104] And although there are many who commit slander, we should not grieve over those who do not judge purely. Instead, let us be consoled by the testimony of our conscience. As Paul has stated, “This is our boast—the testimony of our conscience.”[105] Likewise: “Let each person prove his own work and then he will gain honor for himself alone and not need to depend on another.”[106] In the passage at hand, Solomon commands the people to become less aggravated from slander since we ourselves frequently sin in the same way. For Solomon is simply recounting the common human vices.

[7:23–25]

**“I have tested all things through wisdom.
I said, ‘I will become wise,’ but wisdom withdrew
farther from me.”[107]**

After this, there comes a repetition in the text. Solomon rejects the notion that all human errors can be anticipated and avoided. For it is abundantly clear that even the greatest and wisest of people have erred in significant and tragic ways. In this complaint, we are reminded of

---

[102] Ex. 20:16. The Lutheran tradition divides up the Ten Commandments differently than some other traditions, which might otherwise classify this as the ninth commandment.

[103] Lev. 19:16.

[104] The exact location of this quote is not given. But similar language can be found in Augustine, *Sermon* 355.1.

[105] 2 Cor. 1:12.

[106] Gal. 6:4.

[107] Eccl. 7:23.

our human weakness, prompting us to pray for God to rule over us. As is frequently stated: “I know, Lord, that a person’s way is not in himself.”[108] Likewise: “Commend your way to God; put your hope in him and he will do it.”[109]

[7:26-28]

“I have found a woman more bitter than death which is the hunters’ snare…”[110]

After this, Solomon speaks about women. For whenever our infirmities and misfortunes are told, in some part of this story they include both the faults of women themselves and the passions of men who, on account of women, heap untold misfortunes upon themselves and others, as seen, for instance, in the stories of Samson, David, Paris, and countless other men.

[7:29]

“God has made humankind rightly, but it has preoccupied itself with many questions.”

Solomon is not speaking primarily about creation but instead the kind of actions that God has rightly set up. In other words, God has established an order for all our actions—for instance, how we should eat, drink, be married, serve in a specific calling, and remain within the bounds of our calling. Nonetheless, humankind seeks for fickle deliberations. For example, although David had wives who excelled in beauty and virtue, he craved for another woman.[111] Likewise, although

---

[108] Jer. 10:23.

[109] Ps. 37:5 (Vulgate 36:5). This is one of Melanchthon’s go-to verses when it comes to one’s relationship with God.

[110] Eccl. 7:26.

[111] Melanchthon is referring again to when David seized and had sex with Bathsheba, as told in 2 Sam. 11.

Antony had great authority, he craved for the monarchy.[112] Solomon condemns these errant desires and misplaced wisdom here, as seen in the lives of Pericles, Demosthenes, Brutus, Cicero, and many others who stumbled under the guise of wisdom.[113]

Solomon's saying here is not wrongly applied [more broadly] to [a variety] of teachings. For instance, God has given humankind a sure type of teaching, and God wants our minds to be kept within those boundary markers. However, the deviating nature of humankind is to seek after our fancies and take delight in all manner of speculations as if they were games to be played. Nonetheless, this great evil is strictly condemned in many places of scripture, for instance, in Jeremiah: "I have commanded this: obey me."[114]

---

[112] Melanchthon is probably referring to Marcus Antonius (83-30 BCE), better known as Marc Antony, who ended up fighting Caesar Augustus (Octavian) for rule of Rome in the 30s until he killed himself in recognition of defeat.

[113] This is a list of well-known Greek and Roman rulers. Pericles and Demosthenes were Greek statesmen who lived primarily in Athens in the fifth century and fourth centuries BCE, respectively, while Brutus and Cicero were Roman statesmen who lived in Rome in the first century BCE.

[114] Jer. 7:23.

Ecclesiastes 8

[8:1]

"Human wisdom brightens the face, and the obstinacy will be worthy of hatred."[1]

Although this is a common saying, wisdom does bring happiness since a good conscience is at peace. By contrast, a bad conscience is not only a dreadful internal torture, but it is accompanied by other external punishments such that tyrants will eventually be overcome [by it]. However, it appears that Solomon is specifically speaking here about the topic of the preceding chapter, namely, that wisdom—that is, judgment and choice—brings joy whether it is well used for severity or forbearance, whether there may be struggle or defeat. Meanwhile, a stubborn person, that is, one who has been hardened and does not properly heed warnings but succumbs to the whims of his own wrath, destroys both himself and others. For example, we see evidence of this in the lives of Pericles and Demosthenes, whose stubbornness proved fatal to all of Greece.

[8:2]

"I observe the king's mouth and the words of God's oath."

This saying is very worthy of consideration and remembrance. And it also goes to show quite clearly that although many have interpreted

---

[1] Eccl. 8:1.

it in a foolish manner, this book is not teaching monastic idleness. For Solomon here enduces people to necessary actions and to painful and dangerous conflicts. And lest there be any unrestrained liberty, Solomon places boundaries around how humans should aim to live by ordering obedience to that which has been commanded. For example, Solomon commands us to observe "the king's mouth," by which he means that we are to obey "the king's commandments." He also adds another constraint that we are to obey "God's oath," by which he means "God's law." In fact, Solomon describes these elsewhere as a law of oaths since God has decreed both blesses and curses by means of oaths.[2] Consequently, there is no doubt that crimes will be punished. However, punishments can be lessened for those who repent, which is also included as part of the oath. In short, obedience is best put in the following order: First, we must obey the divine voice, which "the king's mouth" should also be echoing; second, the commands of the king should not conflict with the divine voice. This accords with the following rule: "We must obey God rather than human beings."[3]

Let us now turn to what kind of boundaries have been created for humans as their limits. For example, Solomon writes "...lest there be unrestrained liberty," by which he means that no liberties are granted that prompt us to indulge in evil desires. For instance, we are not to practice idleness or "meddlesomeness."[4] Instead, you are to obey the commandments of God and perform the duties of your vocation as directed by the king, meaning you must not get distracted by undue curiosity, ambition, or whatever evil desire would lead you to wander into other matters. This is why Solomon adds the verse that follows.

---

[2] Both here and in what follows, it appears that Melanchthon may be referring to a passage such as Deuteronomy 28.

[3] Acts 5:29.

[4] In Greek: πολυπραγμοσύνη. See Plato, *Republic* 444b.

[8:3–4]

"Don't be quick to leave his presence..."[5]

That is, "Don't depart from your calling; don't disturb the order of things; don't grasp for power."

"...and don't continue in evil deeds."[6]

That is, "Don't do what you know is forbidden by law." In what follows the second verse, Solomon adds sayings about punishment where at the end he writes, "There is no escaping..."[7] But above he writes that "because the king will do whatever he wants," namely, under the circumstances of God defending legitimate governments. For Solomon is speaking here about legitimate authority or legitimate order. As is stated in Romans 13: "Those who resist authority will face punishment."[8] This doctrine has been repeated elsewhere [in scripture].

[8:5-8]

"The one who keeps the commandments will not face punishment. Wise hearts understand timing and decision making, for there is no circumstance in which these two will not be required. But great is the destruction of the one who does not know the past or the future. A person has authority neither over his own life nor over his own death. Moreover, there is no escaping war, and ungodliness will not save the ungodly."

This passage offers continued preaching on the topic of punishments, and here is the general rule that is handed down: In this life, heinous

[5] Eccl. 8:3a. Melanchthon refers to God, not the king.
[6] Eccl. 8:3b.
[7] Eccl. 8:8.
[8] Rom. 13:2.

sins like murder, perjury, adultery, incestuous lusts, robbery, and so on will be punished with heinous punishments. For instance, as has been written: "The one who takes up the sword will die by the sword."[9] Likewise: "God will judge prostitutes and adulterers."[10] By contrast, God promises a life of peace to those who practice restraint, as seen in this passage: "The one who keeps the commandments will not face punishment."[11]

Solomon then entertains an unstated objection since he knows that punishments are not always immediate, which can encourage many people to act rashly. Consequently, he sets the following sayings to counter their foolish speculation and self-confidence. He says, on the contrary, that "Wise hearts understand timing and decision making."[12] By this he means that punishments will come in due time even if they are delayed for a while. For Solomon is not short-sighted. He knows that every circumstance will be judged. He is not short-sighted; he does not condemn providence, but he knows that divine threats are very real. As Psalm 62 states, "You repay everyone according to his works."[13] Likewise, Psalm 58 says, "There is, indeed, a God who judges people on earth."[14] Similarly, both the law of nature and experience have revealed the same thing to pagans. For instance: "God possesses an avenging eye."[15] Likewise: "God knows how to judge."[16] Also: "Though it delays, punishment will come swiftly."[17] And elsewhere: "He [God] makes up for the delay of punishment by the severity of suffering."[18]

The words that follow next in this passage heap criticism upon short-sighted self-confidence. It is a great shame, Solomon writes,

---

[9] Matt. 26:52.

[10] Heb. 13:4b.

[11] Eccl. 8:5a.

[12] Eccl. 8:5b.

[13] Ps. 62:12 (Vulgate 61:13).

[14] Ps. 58:11 (Vulgate 57:12).

[15] Pseudo-Homer, *The Battle of Frogs and Mice* [*Batrachomyomachia]*, 86 or 97. In Greek: ἔχει θεὸς ἔκδικον ὄμμα.

[16] Theocritus, *Idylls* 23.63. In Greek: θεὸς οἶδε δικάζειν. All translations are my own.

[17] Tibullus, *Elegies* 1.9.4.

[18] Valerius Maximus, *Nine Books of Memorable Deeds and Sayings* 1.1.3.

that people do not give enough thought to the past or to the future, by which he means that although we constantly see horrible examples of punishments, many only laugh in the face of them. And it is about these very examples of punishments from the past that he speaks.

Finally, Solomon then turns to issuing a direct threat. He says that punishments will certainly come and that there is no way for you to prevent or avoid them. For humans do not have life or death in their power, meaning that people can neither extend their lives nor prevent their deaths once God has decided to strike them with punishments. Solomon also says that there is no escaping war, and that ungodliness will certainly be punished. These sayings do not require any further explanation; instead, let us heed the divine voice that threatens punishment upon all who do not repent. As the Lord says in Luke 13, "Unless you repent, you, too, will perish."[19] We must recognize that these thunderbolts are by no means empty noises, instead, we are to be truly terrified at the thought and fear of both present and eternal punishments, which should prompt us to turn to God, to stop living in sin, and to pray to be governed by God, and the like.

[8:9–13]

"Sometimes a person is ruled by another to his own detriment."[20]

Solomon's strong affirmation of providence has already been clearly articulated in which he explicitly stated that crimes would be punished. He now adds objections, which he refutes with an assortment of arguments. In one objection, he mentions how we see criminals oftentimes abound in riches and power while the righteous are oppressed and killed. If providence existed, such injustice would not be tolerated. Solomon recounts this well-known objection here and refutes it by arguing that although criminals oftentimes do flourish while the righteous are oppressed, it is nonetheless most clearly the case that the unrighteous will eventually be punished and that the

19 Lk. 13:3.

20 Eccl. 8:9b.

righteous will fare much better. For instance, David himself lays this objection to rest in Psalm 37: "I have seen the ungodly raised up like the cedars of Lebanon, yet when I passed by them, they were no longer there....For the salvation of the righteous comes from the Lord."[21] And even though for a time, Saul (who banishes David and kills [innocent] priests) rules, Herod kills John the Baptist, and Nero kills Paul, these tyrants are eventually overwhelmed in this life with many punishments.

However, someone may ask: What benefit could possibly arise for good people being killed? This is a question that torments humankind, and it is also something that Solomon deplores. The reason is because the human mind cannot grasp all the reasons why nature is universally subjected to so many sufferings. But the teaching of the church does give the reason: it is due to the existence of sin in all people. Nevertheless, this text, meanwhile, concerns political justice. And so, there is no benefit in criminals committing crimes, for they will be liable to punishment, and here an example of God's providence may be seen. In this way, one part of the objection that Solomon makes regarding the inevitability of judgment may be judged on the basis of reason. Once again, as the poem says it: "Though it delays, punishment will come swiftly."[22]

The other part of the objection that Solomon makes relates to what happens to good people. In short, human wisdom cannot fully judge these things, however, the ultimate deliverance of the righteous has been established in the Word of God, which must be assented to by faith. For instance, righteous people like Abel and John the Baptist knew that God is just, and so they looked forward to the future deliverance and salvation of the Church, to which the resurrection both of the Son of God and the other saints as well as the miracles performed in the Church testify. It is for this reason that Solomon writes elsewhere: "The righteous have hope in death."[23] Similarly, Job says, "Though God slay me, yet I will hope in him."[24] This is how the Church responds to this second objection.

---

[21] Ps. 37:35–36, 39 (Vulgate 36:35–36, 39).

[22] Tibullus, *Elegies* 1.9.4.

[23] Prov. 14:32.

[24] Job 13:15.

Nevertheless, because punishments are delayed, people grow in arrogance and boldness. Consequently, Solomon weaves in this complaint here with full knowledge that correction against evil deeds may not be immediately forthcoming so that the hearts of those who want to do evil deeds are inflamed to do so. It is to this complaint that Solomon again adds to offer an explanation and solution. "Even though evildoers are tolerated for a long time, I am nevertheless aware that it will go well for those who fear God; meanwhile, it will not go well for the ungodly, and their days are numbered, for those who do not fear God will pass away like a shadow." Therefore, Solomon teaches lest, offended by that inequality in this life, we abandon God; instead, let us accept the Word of God, which promises deliverance and salvation to the righteous. By contrast, both scripture and many clear examples testify to punishments that are forthcoming to the ungodly. In this way, there are many sayings among the poets that speak about such punishments. For instance, Claudian writes:

> There is a thought that has often brought doubt to my mind.
> Do the gods care at all about the worlds? Is there any ruler?
> Or do human affairs occur by blind chance?
> But after I had studied the laws and ordinances of the properly ordered world,
> As well as the boundaries of the sea and the ordering of the years,
> And the rotation of days and nights,
> I concluded that everything was arranged according to the direction
> Of a God who ordered the stars to move based on a fixed law,
> And for the crops to grow at the appointed time,
> Who commanded the waxing and waning of the Moon,
> And for the light of the Sun to complement it.
> This God spread the shore before the waves
> And balanced the globe in the middle of its axis.
> Yet when I observed how human affairs became engulfed in darkness,
> With the wicked leading rich and long lives while the godly were tormented,
> My faith and purpose again drew downcast and weakened.
> And I unwillingly began following the philosophy of another,
> Which teaches that atoms drift in an aimless motion,

That new particles float into a vast emptiness,
Where they are guided by chance and not by design,
And which maintains that we can either know nothing of God,
Or that there is no God, or that this God takes no notice of us.
Yet it was Rufinus'[25] punishment that finally resolved this issue
And released the gods from the charge.
Now, therefore, I can no longer complain that the unrighteous
Have reached the highest pinnacle of success.
Instead, they have been lifted high
So that they can crash to the ground with greater force.[26]

[8:14–17]

"Bad things happen to righteous people."

Solomon lingers here on the sermon on providence already begun above, and he repeats the teaching in which the following is asserted: Providence should not be denied even though punishments of evildoers in this life are delayed while oppressions of the righteous are apparent. Indeed, the true refutation of the objection is that there is another judgment coming in which the scales of justice will not be momentary—they will be eternal. Solomon, therefore, comprehends this refutation in his command to fear God by asserting the following: "It will go well for those who fear God."[27] But what human wisdom seeks to understand, namely, why the righteous are often severely oppressed while the wicked flourish is, as Solomon writes,

[25] Flavius Rufinus (c. 335-395) was a statesman who rose to incredible influence as a politician and advisor to Emperor Theodosius I and his son Arcadius. He made many enemies during his tenure, and this entire poem is an invective against him. Rufinus was killed by a Gothic leader as a result of a bad military strategy he advised Emperor Arcadius to make.

[26] Claudius Claudianus, *Against Rufinus* 1.1–2.3. Though a native Greek speaker, Claudianus wrote mostly in Latin poetry. The English translation provided is my own based on the Latin original. Although Melanchthon makes mention of the last phrase in his other writings, it is not typical for him to cite the entire section.

[27] Eccl. 8:12; cf. Sir. 1:19.

"vanity."[28] That is to say, it is a futile endeavor because the wisdom of God is not located in the sharpness of the human mind. Instead, the causes have been revealed in general to the Church as the cause for which it has been subjected to the cross—as it is stated in its proper place.

Consequently, Solomon commands us to abandon this search for human wisdom and instead to abide in the fear of God and to use the present gifts of God—food, drink, and our callings in government and the household—according to the commandments. This is the sum and substance of the long explanation in this very chapter. This question has long tormented the human race. For many, upon observing the favorable circumstances of the wicked in contrast to the unfavorable circumstances of the righteous, conclude that there is no such thing as [divine] providence. Nonetheless, the exceeding strength of faith is not deterred by such spectacles. Rather, it clings to the true knowledge of God and waits for the day of judgment. This same message is frequently repeated in Psalm 36: "Do not imitate evildoers."[29] Indeed, let students consider what both poets and other writers have often discussed when it comes to this matter. Sometimes they express doubts and sometimes they make assertions, for instance, "Be warned: Learn righteousness and do not despise the gods."[30] Similarly, in his book *Rhetoric,* Aristotle offers a saying from Stesichorus: "Do no harm to anyone,"[31] because the cicadas will sing in the fields [not, as they should, from the trees wrongly cut down], meaning that that the poor who labor under oppression in their fields, voice these complaints and move God to punish tyrants.

[28] Eccl. 8:14.

[29] Ps. 36:1.

[30] Virgil, *Aeneid* 6.20.

[31] Aristotle, *Rhetoric* 2.21.8 and 3.11.6. Stesichorus is a Greek lyric poet who lived from c. 630–555 BCE.

Ecclesiastes 9

[9:1-3]

"The righteous and the wise live, and their works are in God's hand. And yet, humankind does not understand the totality of the love and hate that exists in all things before God's presence. No matter whether a person is righteous, evil, good, or pure, all things happen to all people in a similar way, just as there live in the world those who offer sacrifices and those who do not. As it happens to the good person, so it happens to the sinner. And as it happens to the liar, so it happens to those who tell the truth. The fact that the same fate awaits us all is the worst of all things that happens under the sun. And as a result of this, the hearts of the human race are full of evil, and foolishness runs wild in their hearts until they die."[1]

Although this part of the text has been obscured by interpretations that have gone astray, it is quite evident that this complaint has been repeated from the perspective of outward appearance, which motivates many people to deny [divine] providence based solely on the awareness that favorable circumstances happen to the wicked just as unfavorable circumstances happen to the righteous. Consequently, Solomon is preaching here against outward appearance with the purpose of driving us away from it so that we would not judge solely based upon these occurrences. Rather, Solomon is preaching that we should embrace the divine message with the firmest faith. This

---

[1] Eccl. 9:1–3.

message affirms what must be done and that judgment must be expected. This is the essence of Solomon's thinking. For he explicitly condemns here the madness of those who deny providence and insists that such foolishness is fatal to those who deny God based solely on these occurrences or based solely on outward appearance.

Upon establishing the essence of Solomon's thinking on this matter, we now need to refute the interpretation of the monks whose interpretation has been littered across the Church as follows: "No one knows whether he is worthy of love or hate."[2] What the monks fail to understand is that this saying serves as a warning to not judge providence solely on the basis of favorable or unfavorable circumstances. Rather than affirming the truth on this matter from the message of the Gospel, the monks misinterpret this saying by applying this passage to the doubts of the conscience about receiving forgiveness of sins, concerning which it must be derived from the message of the Gospel and not from one's own conscience. Indeed, it is quite evident that the monks badly twist this saying into a cause for doubt. For it is certainly the case that those who commit crimes against the conscience know that they are acting in hatred. For instance, when David took another man's wife, he knew that he was committing a crime that greatly angered God.[3] And although the monks concede that crimes against the conscience elicit God's wrath, they also say that those who have converted are always in a state of doubt when it comes to grace.

It is absolutely crucial to recognize that this fanciful interpretation of the monks is false and godless, and it destroys the nature of the Gospel. For the unmistakable and immovable message of the Gospel is this: Upon repenting of our sins in faith, it is established that our sins are truly forgiven, that we are recipients of grace through the work of [Christ] the Mediator, and that we are freed from doubt. As it says in Ephesians 3: "Through whom we are bold to approach in confidence through the faith of Christ."[4] Likewise in Hebrews: "Having such a high priest, let us approach the throne of grace with confidence."[5]

---

[2] Eccl. 9:1.

[3] 2 Sam. 11.

[4] Eph. 3:12.

[5] Heb. 4:14.

It is necessary to understand that we have certainty on both sides. On the one hand, for example, it is important for David to know the truth that God was greatly angered when he took another man's wife, which wrath was shown when Nathan leveled horrible punishments against him. On the other hand, David later received forgiveness when he repented, which enabled him to extinguish doubt and most assuredly become established again in his receiving of grace, and that by assenting [to Nathan's judgment] and by faith [in forgiveness] he would be able to sustain himself even though living in exile and in great consternation.[6]

To be sure, the monks would object here by stating that based on this reasoning not even the saints could say they please God since they commit sins of ignorance. This is my response: The saints should admit both that they commit sins of ignorance and that they are guilty of many other vices. As David said [to God], "No one alive is justified in your sight."[7] Rather, God is pleased when a person puts faith in [Christ] the Mediator, and that person's uncleanness is covered by the Mediator. As it is written: "There is now no condemnation for those who walk in Christ Jesus."[8] Likewise: "Blessed are those whose iniquities are forgiven and whose sins have been covered."[9] This consolation is the true message of the Gospel.

However, the monks have introduced darkness into the Church by not understanding the difference between Law and Gospel. And this has led them to distort Solomon's words to fit their delusions when all Solomon is saying is this: "We must not judge based on outward appearance," and he leads us to the Word of God. On the contrary, once David heard that he is absolved [of sins], he must judge that he has really been absolved despite the reality that he might still fall victim to great punishments, for the circumstances that follow do illustrate God's wrath. Nonetheless, David must judge from the point

---

[6] This story is told in depth in 2 Samuel 11 and 12. For more Reformation-era interpretations of this passage, see Derek Cooper and Martin Lohrmann, eds., *1–2 Samuel, 1–2 Kings, 1–2 Chronicles* in the Reformation Commentary on Scripture, vol. 5 (Downers Grove, IL: IVP Academic, 2016), 190–210.

[7] Ps. 143:2.

[8] Rom. 8:1.

[9] Ps. 32:1; Rom. 4:7.

of view of God's Word rather than circumstances. Much less should we judge others on the basis of outward appearance. For example, both Saul and Jonathan died in the same way; although human wisdom is incapable of discerning why circumstances occurred in this way, the teaching of the Church is capable of discerning it.[10] For instance, Saul's death agrees with this principle: "Those who draw the sword will die by the sword."[11] Meanwhile, Jonathan's death occurred for other reasons because God had previously testified that he was pleased with Jonathan, indicating that Jonathan and David knew the reasons why the Church was subjected to the cross.[12]

[9:4–6]

"Therefore, what should we choose? There is hope in being alive. For it is better to be a living dog than a dead lion."[13]

We have already witnessed how often the complaint has been repeated that similar things happen to both the righteous and the unrighteous. This is because it is a confounding matter that unsettles our minds and weakens our wills to do what is right. Therefore, Solomon sets the precept over against this offense. Indeed, the truth is that we still must obey God, which is the reason for this question: "Therefore, what should we choose?" In other words, are we still supposed to choose to do what is right even when the rewards do not seem to follow? Here is how Solomon responds: Yes, we must certainly submit to our calling and leave the results to God. As he has stated above so many times, "Commend your way to God, and he will act for you."[14] To be sure, this does not mean that you will be as successful a warrior as Asa was.[15] Or that you will be as successful a commander as Scipio

10 1 Sam. 31.
11 Matt. 26:52.
12 1 Sam. 18:1–3; 20:1–42.
13 Eccl. 9:4.
14 Ps. 37:5.
15 2 Chron. 14:1–5.

was.[16] So, take a lesson from Fabius, which is to say that all you need to do is just attend to your calling.[17] As Paul said, "What is required is for each person to be faithful."[18] Similarly: "Our sufficiency comes from God."[19] Consequently, Solomon writes here that "There is hope in being alive," by which he means that living drives us toward our calling. And when he says that "it is better to be a living dog than a dead lion," he indicates that even though you may not be able to be a lion, you can still be a decent puppy. As such, why are we still searching for lions, that is, heroic commanders and leaders such as Gideon, Samson, and David from days of old?[20] Would it not be better for us to make use of our own callings instead? Even though we cannot be lions as these men were, we can still be like puppies, meaning that we can do something worthwhile, namely, we can pray to God and ask to be made vessels of mercy. Solomon actually dwells on this passage for quite a long time. He teaches us that the dead have already departed from controlling their lives and that we who are alive now can do something worthwhile. Solomon therefore orders us to obey our calling, submit to God in faith and in a good conscience, and accept whatever comes to pass.

---

[16] Publius Cornelius Scipio (ca. 235–183 BC) was a Roman general who earned the epithet *Africanus*, "conqueror of Africa," due to his military successes for Rome during the Second Punic War. There are multiple primary accounts of Scipio's exploits, including Livy's *History of Rome*.

[17] Quintus Fabius Maximus Verrucosus (ca. 280–203 BC) was a Roman general who served as dictator of the Roman Republic from 221 to 217. He was instrumental in the Second Punic War, earning the epithet *Cunctator*, "Delayer," for his delaying tactics. Probably the best primary source on his life is told in Plutarch's *Parallel Lives*.

[18] 1 Cor. 4:2.

[19] 2 Cor. 3:5.

[20] The life of Gideon is told in Judges 6–8, Samson in Judges 13–16, and David in 1 Sam. 16-30 and 1 Kgs. 1-2.

[9:7–10]

"Go and eat your food in joy because your works are pleasing to God."[21]

Solomon says that we are to do these things in accordance with our calling. As he subsequently states, "This is the portion of your life and work that God has given you."[22] And then afterward he adds, "Everything your hand can do, do it earnestly."[23] This saying must be closely followed, for it clearly demonstrates that Solomon does not advocate any sort of withdrawal from common society or from everyday interactions, but neither does he advocate the idle lifestyle of monks. Instead, Solomon presents a very serious doctrine and admonition here by ordering us to obey our calling earnestly and to entrust our results to God, which requires steadfast faith and diligence. As he says, "Do it earnestly."[24] He then adds the sweetest consolation, namely, that the godly should recognize that following such a course of action is in accordance with their calling to please God and is divinely controlled even though we will encounter many impediments and misfortunes along the way. However, another objection is added immediately.

[9:11a]

"What is the point of work if victory is not determined by speed or strength?"[25]

Here is my response: I want people to work, but I also want them not to trust in their own wisdom or strength. Nor do I want them to attempt unnecessary things based purely on their confidence in how wise or strong they are. Instead, I want them to ask and hope

21 Eccl. 9:7.
22 Eccl. 9:9.
23 Eccl. 9:10.
24 Eccl. 9:10.
25 Eccl. 9:11a.

for God's assistance regardless of the results, resisting the urge to abandon God or bristle against him but rather to acknowledge him in our weakness. This mindset accords with the following saying: "I know, Lord, that a person's way is not his own."[26] Likewise: "A person can do nothing unless given to him from heaven."[27] As has been amply discussed, these words refer to outcomes; they do not imply that there is absolutely no freedom in the actual choice of our will [to do something of our own choosing].

[9:11b–14]

"Time and chance happen to all."[28]

This verse agrees with another saying: "Unless the Lord builds the house, those who build it labor in vain."[29] First God wills something. Then follows the success of human plans since it is God who ultimately sustains them, blesses them, and governs them. For we should not understand time and chance in an Epicurean way.[30] On the contrary, Solomon condemns placing confidence in our human strength and intellect, both of which imagine themselves to be completely self-sufficient and without the need of God. This is why Solomon immediately follows this saying with a warning about human weakness: "Like a fish that has been caught, no one knows when his hour will come."[31] People have a tendency to construe good fortune through a false sense of assumptions and in a foolish and unfounded hope, but this will all fall apart when faced with actual calamities, as seen in the lives of Marius, Pompey, Julius [Caesar],[32]

---

[26] Jer. 10:23.

[27] John 3:27.

[28] Eccl. 9:11b.

[29] Ps. 127:1 (Vulgate 126:1).

[30] In general, Epicureanism rejects the belief of divine involvement in human affairs.

[31] Eccl. 9:12.

[32] These were three notable Roman statesmen and military commanders living in the first-century BC.

and countless others who ventured beyond their callings. In fact, there are common sayings dealing directly with this. For instance: "Every human thing hangs by a thin thread, and that which used to have value loses it in the blink of an eye."[33] Similarly: "Vain people do vain things in accord with their own desires."[34] I must also repeat the saying that I have repeated so often before: "Commend your way to God, and hope in him, and he will act for you."[35] That is, do what is necessary according to your calling, seek out and hope for God's assistance, and remember that you have weaknesses.

[9:15–18]

"There was once a poor yet wise person who delivered a city...and one evildoer will destroy many good things."[36]

It is highly beneficial in life to ponder what I mentioned above, namely, that there are two kinds of people in this world: those who are "vessels of wrath" and those who are "vessels of mercy."[37] First, those who are "vessels of wrath" are miserable souls who are destructive both to themselves and others despite the fact that they can also sometimes embody greatness and wisdom. As Solon once said, "Governments are overthrown by those with great and surpassing talents."[38] Examples of such vessels of wrath are Achan, Zedekiah, Catiline, [Marc] Antony, and many others, while, in the Church, such examples include [Paul of] Samosata, Arius, Mani, and many other destructive theologians. Regarding all such things, Solomon says this:

---

[33] Ovid, *Letters from the Black Sea*, 4.3.35–36. This is my translation based on the Latin original.

[34] In Greek: μάταιοι μάταια λογίζονται δι ἐπιθυμίας. All translations are my own.

[35] Ps. 37:5.

[36] Eccl. 9:15 and 9:18.

[37] Rom. 9:22–23.

[38] Solon (c. 630–c. 560 BC) who was an Athenian politician and author whose writings have only survived in fragments from subsequent authors.

"One evildoer will destroy many good things." Or to quote the same concept in Greek literature: "Oftentimes an entire city is punished for one person's wickedness."[39]

Second, those who are "vessels of mercy" are pleasant souls who are edifying both to themselves and others. Examples include Samuel, David, and Jeremiah. In fact, this poor yet wise person that Solomon mentions here describes people just like Jeremiah. For even though nobody listened to Jeremiah during the tumultuous events taking place in his lifetime, he nevertheless preserved the Church.[40] Upon considering this, each one of us should pray with constant groans that God would make us vessels of mercy and that God would protect us from becoming damaging contagions that infect the human race. As the prophets proclaim in Psalms, "Look upon your servants and direct the work of our hands."[41] Likewise, we see in Isaiah, "You, Lord, are our Father. We are your clay, and you form us. We are all the work of your hands. Do not become overly angry."[42]

Alongside what Solomon discusses above, he also summarizes what follows as indicating that good counsel is heard by only a few while bad counsel is welcomed by many. This, therefore, leads him to conclude that "the words of the poor are held in contempt" and "the words of the wise are held in silence."[43] What this means is that only those who seek the truth and seek those things that are beneficial actually listen to the words of the poor and wise; those who are consumed with covetousness do not. This corresponds to what Solomon wrote elsewhere: "It is better to happen upon a bear robbed of her cubs than a fool bent on his foolishness."[44] What this means is that it is very difficult to reason with someone who is consumed with covetousness or enamored with foolishness.

---

[39] Hesiod, *Works and Days* 240. In Greek: πολλάκι καὶ ξύμπασα πόλις κακοῦ ἀνδρός ἀπηύρα. All translations are my own.

[40] See especially Jer. 18, which illustrates the metaphor of a vessel (or pot) and the people refusing to listen to Jeremiah.

[41] Ps. 90:16–17 (Vulgate 89:16-17).

[42] Isa. 64:8–9.

[43] Eccl. 9:16–17.

[44] Prov. 17:12.

Ecclesiastes 10

[10:1a]

"Dead flies spoil perfume's sweetness."[1]

What Solomon means here is that good counsel, trustworthy doctrine, and the well-established arts are corrupted on a daily basis by busybodies who are more loudly heard in government halls and among the people than are humble and poor people who teach what is right and who give beneficial counsel.

[10:1b–10:3]

"Foolishness is better than wisdom and fame—for a while."[2]

This saying agrees with another: "He did not put rumors above safety."[3] Although Fabius was regarded as a fool for a while, subsequent

[1] Eccl. 10:1a.

[2] Eccl. 10:1b.

[3] Quintus Fabius Maximus Verrucosus (ca. 280–203 BC) was a Roman statesman and general. He served as dictator of the Roman Republic from 221 to 217. He was instrumental in the Second Punic War against Hannibal, where he earned the epithet *Cunctator*, "Delayer," for his delaying tactics against the famous general Hannibal, who led Carthage's army in Rome. Melanchthon is probably referring to a story from Plutarch about the Master of Horse. In *Parallel Lives* 3.5.4, Plutarch tells the story of Fabius's master of the horse, an officer named Minucius, who disagreed with Fabius's delaying tactics and openly ridiculed him. The office of master of horse, *magister equitum*, was an

events demonstrated that his plans were sound. This agrees with the saying, "The hearts of the wise are in their right hand," which occurs when we hold things more firmly with the result that we do not succumb to anger, distress, or ambition. By contrast, "The hearts of fools are in their left hand," that is, such heats are held more feebly with the result that they rush toward anger, lust for fame, and allow distress and other emotions to drive them. A rule about propriety is handed down here that is universally connected to a false sense of wisdom, namely, that all people who are arrogant and admire themselves while they simultaneously despise others and judge them to be fools, much like how Epicureans and hypocrites believe the Apostles to be insane. A similar example can be found in the life of Pompey, who thought that those who attempted to dissuade him from war were wrong.[4]

[10:4–7]

"If someone stronger prevails over you, do not give up your place. For healing will cause great sinners to cease their ways."[5]

Even if the antagonists, the sycophants, and the conceited braggarts of the world prevail for a while, the person who aspires to righteousness will not be moved to abandon his station in life on account of the perversity of those who judge them or on account of distress. For example, a good and faithful pastor should not be moved by the slanders and complaints of the people to desert the Church, abandon his convictions, or give in to unrighteousness actions. This is because the pastor is able to bring about a great deal of healing in a short amount of time.

What follows next in this passage is a complaint that laments this common evil in which fools and wicked people are often in charge,

---

important one in the Roman Republic who held *imperium*, or "ruling authority," but only through appointment by the Roman dictator—in this case, Fabius.

[4] Gnaeus Pompeius Magnus (106-48 BC), better known as Pompey, was defeated by Julius Caesar at the Battle of Pharsalus.

[5] Eccl. 10:4.

with the result that those who enjoy positions of leadership and who flatter the lord are more popular than those who are wise and who offer faithful counsel. As the following verse proclaims:

> They say that life is greatly alluring to the perverse
> And that the flatterer prospers best of all,
> Followed second by the sycophant
> [And third by the wicked.][6]

[10:8a]

"Whoever digs a pit will fall into it."[7]

These sayings about punishments correspond to the above laments, which warn us that unfortunate outcomes are the result of bad decisions. This accords with a rule I have often repeated: "Severe offenses are punished with severe punishments in this life." Likewise: "The measure you use to judge others will be the same measure used to judge you."[8] This is why Solomon says, "Whoever digs a pit will fall into it." It agrees with many common sayings, including these Greek ones: "Poor counsel goes most poorly for the one who counsels it."[9] And likewise: "The one who causes evil for another causes evil to himself."[10]

---

[6] Menander originally uttered these words, but most of his writings only survive in fragments. Portions of this saying appear in Euripides, *Hippolytus* 426. Hippolytus was the illegitimate son of King Theseus of Athens and Queen Hippolyta of the Amazons. In Greek: ὁ βίος μάλιστα τοῖς πονηροῖς ἥδεταί πράττει δ' ὁ κόλαξ ἄριστα πάντων δεύτερος ὁ συκοφάντης. All translations are my own.

[7] Eccl. 10:8a.

[8] Lk. 6:38.

[9] Hesiod, *Works and Days* 266. In Greek: ἡ δὲ κακὴ βουλὴ τῷ βουλεύσαντι κακίστη. All translations are my own.

[10] Callimachus, *Aetia* fragment 2.5. Though originally containing several thousand lines, this poem only survives in fragments. In Greek: τεύχων ὡς ἑτέρῳ τις ἑῷ κακὸν ἥπατι τεύχει. All translations are my own. Literally, the

[10:8b]

"Whoever tears down a wall will be bitten by a snake."[11]

This is a specific punishment that applies to those who seek to reform governments. In Greek, they are called *overzealous*,[12] that is, those who seek unsolicited change. Generally speaking, these kinds of leaders are eventually overtaken by the impertinence of those whose reins they have loosened. For example, Julius [Caesar] was killed by his own countrymen, and so what was said about Julius [Caesar] often truly happens: "I saved these men only to be murdered by them."[13] What Solomon's saying means, therefore, is that the political "wall" had only been partly constructed. For there are "snakes" who will insolently take advantage of the freedom they receive from another's diligence.

[10:9]

"Whoever removes stones will be crushed by them."[14]

This is a common figure of speech. It means that those who remove stones are like those who attempt to alter the laws and structure of the government. It agrees with the previous saying that great dangers will fall upon the one who attempts to reform the structure of the government—whether attempted either by invoking divine authority or through human overzealousness or ambition. But then the results will be far worse, as we see, for example, in the lives of Brutus, Casius, and

word ἧπαρ (in this instance, ἥπατι) means "liver," but it generally referred to the core of a person in antiquity.

[11] Eccl. 10:8b.

[12] Here Melanchthon uses the Greek term πολυπραγμοσύνη, which translates to something like "one who conducts too much business." It carries connotations, however, of someone who is a busybody, officious, or meddlesome.

[13] Suetonius, *The Twelve Caesars* 1.84.

[14] Eccl. 10:9a.

Antony. In this way, we must always keep this saying of Pindar in view: "It is easy to disturb a city, but to reestablish peace is from God alone."[15]

The example that follows this one is more generic: "Whoever cuts logs will be wounded by them."[16] What this means is that whoever forms or fosters the various talents of a people or students, such as preachers and teachers do, will regularly be injured by them.

[10:10]

"Just as a dull blade is sharpened again only through great labor, so wisdom accompanies great effort."[17]

This is a precept about diligence in action and endurance amid many obstacles. It parallels an ancient saying: "We learn from the things we suffer."[18] In this precept, Solomon criticizes those who are lazy in their responsibilities, urging instead vigilance, care, effort, and serious intention, as is commanded in many other sayings. For example, Christ admonished the lazy servant who had gained nothing from his talent.[19] In fact, there are many such examples commanding diligence in all kinds of ancient writings. There are similar sayings in other ancient writings. For instance, "Life gives nothing to humanity without hard work."[20] Epicharmus wrote likewise: "The gods sell us every good thing at the price of pain."[21] And Hesiod stated something similar, "Diligence increases our workload."[22] In

---

[15] Pindar (c. 518–c. 438 BC) was a Greek poet. Melanchthon's quotation comes from the Latin, however. The exact source of this quote from Pindar is not known.

[16] Eccl. 10:9b.

[17] Eccl. 10:10.

[18] This is a saying from Aesop. It rhymes in Greek: παθήματα μαθήματα.

[19] Matt. 25:14–30. Melanchthon is referring to the third servant who hid the talent in the ground.

[20] Horace, *Satire* 1.9 line 59.

[21] Epicharmus, fragment 36. In Greek: τῶν πόνων πωλοῦσιν πάντα ἡμῖν αγαθὰ θεοὶ. All translations are my own.

[22] Hesiod, *Works and Days* 412. In Greek: μελετὴ δὲ ἔργον τε ὀφείλει. All translations are my own.

short, we must be diligent in performing the duties of our calling and doing those things which are necessary. We must guard against becoming so overly curious[23] that we are tempted to go beyond our calling, just as a hunting dog becomes useless when it gets distracted and immediately loses sight of its prey. And the saying of Seneca is well-known: "We are ignorant of necessary things because we do not learn necessary things."[24]

[10:10–11]

"Slanderers are like snakes that bite without warning."[25]

This saying agrees what was said above, namely, that "slander[26] troubles the wise and destroys their noble heart."[27] Slander is an utterly savage pestilence that is the spark for great dissensions out of which arise religious disputes, wars, and catastrophes. Accordingly, Moses ordered the following precept: "Do not spread slander among the people."[28] Therefore, the whole class of people who slander and detract is condemned.

[10:12–14]

"Words from the lips of the wise are gracious..."[29]

Solomon distinguishes wise counselors and teachers from fools who have the appearance of wisdom but actually do not possess it since

---

[23] In Greek: πολυπραγμοσύνη.

[24] Seneca [the Younger], *Moral Epistles* 45.4. Martin Luther uses this same quote in his lectures on Romans (WA 371.16).

[25] Eccl. 10:11.

[26] The Latin word *calumnia* can be translated in various ways: "deceit," "trickery," "lying," "pretense," "false accusation," "slander," "extortion," "bribery," "trouble," "evasion," and "calumny."

[27] Eccl. 7:7. The Latin version differs slightly from more modern versions.

[28] Lev. 19:16.

[29] Eccl. 10:12.

they do not direct their plans toward a standard principle, instead being guided by either their own blind emotions or those of others—similar to how Mardonius foolishly advised Xerxes[30] to enter war or how Pompey [foolishly] listened to instigators.[31] Solomon says that these kinds of people are ignorant of what has happened before, by which he means that they do not learn from past examples that illustrate how people who listen to foolish advice or accept dangerous teaching end up destroying both themselves and others. Nor do they anticipate the punishments that follow as a result.

[10:15]

"The labor of fools torments them because they do not know the way to the city."[32]

Here is what Solomon means. These people who are supposedly "wise" perversely try to accomplish many things—but all in vain. For instance, they try to reform too many things, they summon misfortunes both on themselves and others, they do not listen to other people's points of view, they do not consider the circumstances of the moment, and they do not know what should be done. This is what Solomon means when he writes, "they do not know the way to the city." In fact, we could substitute the city for "the courts," as is described in the story of a shepherd who had been given a mirror in the court. After contemplating himself in the mirror, he was

[30] According to Herodotus, the Persian general Mardonius (d. 479 BC) encouraged King Xerxes I (c. 519-465 BC) to invade Greece. See Herodotus, *The Histories* 7.9.

[31] Pompey (106–48 BC) listened to the advice of his counselors and reluctantly agreed to enter into battle with Julius Caesar at the Battle of Pharsalus in 48 BC. Though outnumbered, Caesar's army soundly defeated Pompey's. Pompey was pressured into war by senators and military officers. For instance, as Cicero stated in his *Epistles to Friends* 7.3.2, "from that time onward that incredible man [Pompey] was no general." In Latin: *ex eo tempore vir ille summus nullus imperator fuit*. All translations are my own. See also Plutarch, *Cato the Younger* 55.

[32] Eccl. 10:15.

made more insolent by admiring his face. But subsequently, as told by Francesco Petrarch, he fell into punishments: "That wretch moans forever to the shepherds of the court who first gave bad gifts!"[33]

[10:16–20]

"Woe to the land whose king is a child and whose princes eat in the morning."[34]

This is a very clear precept. In fact, Solomon is not just speaking about those who are young in age; he is also speaking about those who are old in age who always lived in a state of leisure and pleasure and who were? never made more cautious from teaching, from the vicissitudes of life, or from life experience. For whenever rulers take as their primary aim the pleasures of the body, they begin neglecting their legal, executive, and military duties. This is exactly how the men who sought Penelope's hand in marriage acted—they were born to feast on the land.[35] This is the exact opposite of that which Polybius cites from Hesiod: "The sons of Aeacus have indulged in war as in a feast."[36]

---

[33] Francesco Petrarch, *Bucolic Poems* 6.158.-159. Petrarch's collection of poems here were published in 1357. All translations are my own.

[34] Eccl. 10:16.

[35] In Homer's *Odyssey*, Penelope has to faithfully wait for her husband Odysseus, who has been away from home for twenty years, while other male suitors try to pressure her to re-marry. As they wait, they become freeloaders and rapacious guests.

[36] Polybius, *Histories* 5.2. Aeacus was a mythological king in ancient Greece.

Ecclesiastes 11

[11:1–2]

"Cast your bread upon the waters."[1]

The entirety of this chapter is the light of this whole book. For it shows that in these sermons, proof of the position about providence has been established and that a refutation of arguments, to which people are moved by nature, would doubt providence. In this way, this notion here is found in the end of the book as follows: "At the end of all things, God will bring you into judgment."[2] In fact, Solomon expressly confirms that God both presently judges and will continue to judge the deeds of humankind, going so far as to repeat this assertion at the end of this book: "Fear God and keep his commandments."[3]

Consequently, having established this notion that God is going to judge and that we must obey God according to his commandments, consolation now follows. In short, when our mind entertains doubt, what am I to do? For instance, I concede that many of our labors are in vain and that many are thankless. I also concede how frequently hardships and difficulties arise in our lives. Should these things, then, compel me to abandon society, withdraw myself into solitude, and follow the old adage that we should therefore "live in obscurity"[4]? Not at all. On the contrary, all these things should com-

---

[1] Eccl. 11:1.

[2] Eccl. 12:14.

[3] Eccl. 12:13.

[4] In Greek: λάθε βιώσας. This is a saying from Epicurus in which he encouraged people to live a life free from politics, free from seeking status, and free from drawing unnecessary attention to oneself.

pel us to do what was stated above: Be strong in the work that God has assigned you.[5] Consequently, Solomon now says this: Obey God's commandments and leave the results to him. Meanwhile, do not become crushed with grief if the opposite of what you want to happen occurs; rather, if this happens, you must still obey God, so that by faith you may hold on to tranquility, prayer, and hope. May you come to know that you please God in your obedience to him, your labors will never completely be in vain—even if intense misfortunes come your way in the process, as, for example, when great rebellions disturbed Moses's rule or when David's son was moved to commit sedition against him.[6] Adversities such as these come about so that we do not lose hope, abandon peace of mind, or forsake prayer or other duties that the Lord has commanded. Instead, we are to return to that which we frequently cite: "Commend your way to the Lord; trust in him and he will do this."[7] Likewise, Paul said, "Your work in the Lord will not be in vain."[8] And Psalm 1: "Their leaves will not wither."[9] All recognize that all this teaching and consolation in life is extremely necessary; in fact, it clearly comes from God, for we know that reason finds offense at this kind of confusion and has serious doubts about divine providence and assistance. This is not only the centerpiece of this chapter but also the centerpiece of this entire book.

What Solomon is referring to when he says to "Cast your bread upon the waters" has to do with works of governing. That is, it is the duty of a teacher to scatter knowledge among students as if he were casting bread into the water to feed fish or tossing seed into the field to produce crops. A [political] leader should perform their duties in the same way. For although some of our labors will show no results, other labors will benefit other people and, in fact, their fruits will be seen by later generations. For instance, Jeremiah's leadership was full of trouble, but it still benefitted all later generations. In a word, may

---

[5] Here Melanchthon is summarizing his explanation of the first section of the previous chapter.

[6] Rebellion against Moses arose in Exodus 16 and Numbers 16, and Absalom's rebellion against David is narrated in 2 Samuel 15.

[7] Ps. 37:5 (Vulgate 36:5).

[8] 1 Cor. 15:58.

[9] Ps. 1:3.

you make the most of every opportunity you have by performing the duties of your calling. This is exactly what Paul meant when he wrote that we "must make the most of every opportunity since the days are evil,"[10] for even the best of plans can often be hindered by setbacks.

[11:3–5]

"When the clouds get full, they will rain down water."[11]

This section combines consolations with warnings. For example, what Solomon means when he writes that "When the clouds get full, they will rain down water," is that you are not in complete control of the circumstances that come your way, and so you must wisely bear for a time whatever happens. Using the analogy of weather for shifts in fortune, sometimes it rains, and sometimes it is blue skies. For instance, during the time of Moses, "the clouds got full," that is, they indicated that it was now time for the people to be taken out of Egypt.[12] In addition, "the clouds got full" as well during the time of Jeremiah, that is, the clouds were filled with sin, which brought down rain and exile among the people.[13] Once an event is set in motion, what happens next cannot be stopped.

The next part of this verse, "Where a tree falls, there it lies,"[14] agrees with that old Greek saying: "That which has been done can no longer be undone."[15] What Solomon means is that we are not in control of our circumstances and so we must have wisdom to know how to respond to them. Solomon dwells on this passage for some time. He states, in short, that the one who demands everything to happen

---

[10] Eph. 5:16.

[11] Eccl. 11:3.

[12] The Israelite's exodus out of Egypt is told in Exodus 3 to 15.

[13] This is one of the primary themes of the entire book of Jeremiah.

[14] Eccl. 11:3b.

[15] Pseudo-Phocylides 56. This is an ancient Greek document originally thought to have been written by Phocylides in the sixth century BC but later regarded as apocryphal. It was a popular textbook during Melanchthon's time and consisted of aphorisms teaching moral lessons. In Greek: οὐ πότε γὰρ δύναται τὸ τετυγμένος γὰρ δύναται τὸ ἄτυκτον.

seamlessly and perfectly will end up doing nothing. Therefore, he writes, "The one who waits for perfect weather will never plant."[16] Solomon then adds a warning that not all circumstances can be foreseen, just as Herodotus of old said the same thing: "It is not clear in the beginning what the outcome will be."[17] Solomon very wisely uses the metaphor of a human fetus to describe this phenomenon. For instance, just as we do not perfectly understand how a baby is formed in a mother's womb, so we cannot presume to know all circumstances that will occur in the future. Nonetheless, this is a source of consolation that Solomon adds, for in this image God clearly cares for the fetus, the pregnant mother is preserved, life is given to the unborn child when still inside the womb, nourishing food is created in the mother's breasts, and the mother's birth canal is miraculously opened when it is time for the baby to be born. In this way, we must recognize that all our life is under God's protection—just as it is written: "In God we live and move and have our being."[18] Indeed, we may safely say that the human race is preserved in many great dangers by God and not by secondary causes. As it is said: "All the hairs on your head are numbered."[19]

[11:6–10]

"Plant your seed in the morning and in the evening..."[20]

In this section, Solomon repeats previous warnings and consolations and also manages to weave in a sermon on death and judgment. He writes, in short, that you should not become discouraged even in the face of the adversities that hinder you, but, instead, you should do what you have been called to do. And when he says, "may you plant your seed in the morning and in the evening," he means what

[16] Eccl. 11:4.

[17] Herodotus *Histories* 7.51.3. In Greek: μὴ ἅμα ἀρχῇ πᾶν τέλος καταφαίνεσθαι.

[18] Acts 17:28.

[19] Matt. 10:30; Luke 12:7.

[20] Eccl. 11:6.

Paul also says: "Make the most of every opportunity since the days are evil."[21] That is to say, when you encounter great obstacles, you must find ways to increase your earnings, help the Church, and teach sound doctrine and the like. After this warning, Solomon then adds the consolation, "Light is sweet…and rejoice in your youth,"[22] and so on, which is to say that, as long as God allows, you should use your gifts reverently, but when God decides to allow adversity, you must practice patient obedience and find solace in him. As Paul said, "Let the peace of God rule in your hearts."[23] Likewise, "I will bear the anger of the Lord and remain in the darkness, for the Lord is my light."[24]

[21] Eph. 5:16.
[22] Eccl. 11:7, 9.
[23] Col. 3:15.
[24] Mic. 7:9.

Ecclesiastes 12

[12:1–5]

"Remember your Creator."[1]

Regardless of whether you encounter favorable or unfavorable circumstances, may you remember your Creator, may you obey him, and may you rest in him. And may you know by faith according to his promises, which he has handed down in his infinite goodness through the Mediator of the Church [Jesus Christ], that he truly hears those who pray to him and who want to obey him and horribly punishes those who oppose him. Consequently, Solomon repeatedly reminds us of God's judgment, making mention of old age and death as a way to bolster his argument for providence and exhort us to fear God, to have faith in him, and to practice obedience. In short, do not carelessly abandon God, for both sickness and death are a constant reminder of our frailty. And even if you were to become drunk in the excess of fortune and aspire to greatness, you must recognize that these idle dreams will still suddenly come crashing down at the hour of our death. For if you condemn God's judgment, you will fall headlong into eternal wrath and eternal punishments. Consequently, to warn against this and to draw us out of our fleshly pride and doubts, Solomon seeks to remind us of our death and judgment as a way to commend us toward providence, fear of God, faith, and obedience. He does this by offering a vivid description of old age that he has taken from his observation of nature itself and from our physical maladies as we age. Still, not all the metaphors he uses are perfectly understood.

---

[1] Eccl. 12:1.

"Before the sun and the moon and the stars grow dark."[2]

Here he means that all of nature appears duller and sadder to the elderly.

"And the clouds return after the rain."[3]

Here he means that new hardships and new adversities are always around the corner. Even when something bad happens, something else always follows. The poet Homer offers the same lament: "And so, evil upon evil me follows me forever."[4] Similarly: "Fear old age, for it never comes alone."[5]

"Those who guard the house tremble."[6]

Here he is referring to the hand, meaning that the nerves, tendons, and ligaments become weaker and feebler.

"Those who are strong fall asleep."[7]

Here he is referring to the legs and feet.

---

2 Eccl. 12:2a.

3 Eccl. 12:2b.

4 Homer, *Iliad* 2.19.290. In Greek: ὡς μοὶ δέχεται κακὸν ἐκ κακοῦ αἰεί.

5 This well-known saying comes from Menander, most of whose writings only exist in fragments. This saying is listed in *Monosticha* (*Sententia*) 802. In something of an exception, Melanchthon provides both the original Greek [φοβοῦ τὸ γῆρας, οὐ γὰρ ἔρχεται μόνον] and a Latin translation.

6 Eccl. 12:3a.

7 Eccl. 12:3b.

"Those who mill will become more sluggish and more tattered."[8]

Here he means that the teeth will become weaker and will fall out.

"Those who watch through the windows will grow dim."[9]

Here he means that the eyes will grow dimmer.

"The doors will close."[10]

Here he means that the lips will become dry and droopy.

"They rise at the sound of birds."[11]

Here he means that sleep will become shorter and that the elderly will be easily awakened by the crowing of the rooster.

"The daughters of music will grow faint."[12]

Here he means either that the ears will grow deaf or that the vocal cords will shrivel up, for in old age our heart beats slower and the lungs and the trachea become weaker in both warmer and colder temperatures.

---

8 Eccl. 12:3c.
9 Eccl. 12:3d.
10 Eccl. 12:4a.
11 Eccl. 12:4c.
12 Eccl. 12:4d.

"They will become afraid of heights."[13]

Here he means that the head will become light from dizziness.

"The almond tree will bloom."[14]

Here he means that the hair will become as gray as an almond tree when ripe.

"The grasshoppers will lose their bounce."[15]

Here he means that the shoulders and hips will droop and that the elderly will walk slouched over. The shape of the shoulders will become more prominently hunched, while the hips and backbone will start to resemble a grasshopper.

"Desire is extinguished."[16]

Here he means that food, drink, and other pleasures will begin to cause indigestion and irritation. For when all our vigor for life is sapped, eating and cooking well goes with it, which leads to poor digestion, poor circulation, and poor nutrition.

Now that Solomon has adequately discussed the exterior, he now turns to the interior.

---

[13] Eccl. 12:5a.
[14] Eccl. 12:5c.
[15] Eccl. 12:5d.
[16] Eccl. 12:5e.

[12:6–12]

"Before the silver cord is snapped."[17]

Here I believe that Solomon is referring to the nerves, tendons, and ligaments since they are similar to white hair follicles. And because they enable cognition and movement, they are very important to the human body.

"And before the golden fountain is emptied."[18]

Here he is referring to the heart, which is the fountain and source of all our strength and circulation of blood.

"And the pitcher is broken over the fountain."[19]

Here he is referring to the artery above the liver. For when Solomon refers to these two related things—a fountain and a pitcher—I take the first as referring to the heart and the second as referring to the artery between the heart and liver. This is because the image of gold is more fitting for the heart and spirit. Consequently, the pitcher can be understood, so to speak, as referring to the fountain of the artery, which draws blood from the liver before then transporting it to the whole body, and so it most truly represents the source of health and wellbeing for the entirety of the body. In fact, it is fitting that Solomon does not neglect mentioning the function of the arteries, which are especially important in supplying our whole body with the nutrients it needs, for it distributes blood throughout the entirety of the body with remarkable precision—and as physical evidence of God's providence.

---

[17] Eccl. 12:6a.
[18] Eccl. 12:6b.
[19] Eccl. 12:6c.

"And the pulley is broken over the well."[20]

Here I believe that Solomon is referring to the stomach when he mentions a well. For this term suggests a deep chamber, while the "pulley" above the stomach refers to nearby organs, namely, the intestines, which are located inside the body like hinges or discs, with the abdominal cavity acting like a kind of pulley system in which the intestines are enclosed.

In short, Solomon offers this extended analogy of old age and death here as a way to remind readers of future judgment, which concept he often repeats: Because God will bring everyone into judgment, he wants by understanding this judgment for faith in God's providence to be confirmed, for fear of God to be aroused, and for prayers and concerns to be given to him in the right manner. Because the terror of eternal wrath, divine abandonment, and horrible torture will last for eternity, the one who guides the religious mind is not slow. This sums up the entire chapter.

[12:13-14]

**"Fear God and keep his commandments.
This is the chief concern for all human beings."[21]**

This saying epitomizes all worship and all obedience, for it leads us to this true God who revealed himself to the people of Israel and who delivered to them both the promises and the law, which were confirmed by unmistakable and unfailing testimonies. This God wants to be acknowledged, obeyed, invoked, and worshiped in accordance with the same message he delivered to the people, which ought to serve as a standard for all our thoughts and actions, namely, to contemplate God and what he teaches, not to deviate from his standards, and may you recognize that those who do so will certainly end up in darkness, in snares of the devil and in the harshest punishments. As such, you should direct all your plans and actions toward the singular

[20] Eccl. 12:6d.

[21] Eccl. 12:13b.

goal of obeying and glorifying God. What is more, you should also keep this rule in mind when judging doctrine and when determining what debates, teachings, and disputes either deviate from the Word of God or do not encourage the cultivation of a mindset that fears God or promotes faith. For there always have been, there always are, and there always will be plenty of Epicureans, pleasure-seeking, worthless opinions, and idolatrous worship. All such things must be examined and avoided with the utmost vigilance. In fact, Solomon's teachings in this book address this very topic, which is a summary of the universal teaching in the Church. It is stated in many places: "Blessed are those who hear the Word of God and keep it."[22] Likewise, we see it epitomized in that whole psalm that begins: "Blessed are those whose ways are blameless and who walk according to the law of the Lord."[23] Also: "If you love me, you will keep my word. My Father will love him, and we will come to him and make our home with him."[24] Once again, this is the same topic that Solomon addresses in many of his sayings in this book.

[22] Luke 11:28.
[23] Psalm 119:1.
[24] John 14:23.

Conclusion

Following the example of Solomon, I will now proceed to repeat the argument and summary of this book here at the end [of this commentary]. What Solomon primarily seeks to do in this book is make a clear case for God's providence. This, secondly, entails refuting all possible objections to it. For instance, Solomon makes his case for providence knowing full well that we experience great and regular misfortunes in life, that evil people are in the majority, that there are few and far between who rightly acknowledge and fear God, that evil people abound in status and wealth, that so many of the godly are afflicted and even killed by evildoers, that faithful leadership brings about little change, and that everything seems to come about by chance.

Here is what Solomon says in response: Despite the great and regular misfortunes that you may experience in life, you should nevertheless be guided by the Word of God, maintain a strong faith in God's providence, not allow occasional adversities to separate you from God, not discard fear of God and a quiet faith in God, and not abandon your calling. In short, do not assume that human tragedy and divine providence are mutually exclusive. For judgment is coming when God will take away this confusion, and all who are evil will be cast into eternal punishment while those who are righteous will prosper. In fact, even in this life, God keeps confusing misfortunes in check, punishes severe crimes, ensures that the government is not completely ineffective, builds for himself the eternal Church, and preserves certain structures of the state and household. Indeed, this is a clear witness to God's presence. For even when the weakness of human nature seems at its worst and the madness of humankind at its maximum, we nonetheless observe the miraculous preservation of the Church of God and some of its hospitable structures. As a result, the contention that human tragedy invalidates providence is inaccurate, as this saying clearly states: "Because so many things happen in a disordered fashion in this life, everything must always be disordered."[1]

The conclusion [of this syllogism] must be rejected. For certainly this confusing misfortune will one day be taken away, and even in this life many things happen in an orderly fashion. For instance, the whole structure of the world is most beautifully ordered and arranged. This includes the shape and position of the sky, air, water, and land, the movement of the stars, the changing of the seasons, the fruitfulness of the earth, the nourishment of the human body, the preservation of the various species, generation of life, the mind's rules for knowing, the preservation of society, and the punishment of severe crimes.

These regulations and ordinances, therefore, must be set in contrast to these confusing misfortunes. Even more, divine revelation itself—by which the Word, the Law, the threats, and the Gospel and promises have been published—must be set in opposition to every difficult event we might otherwise observe. Rather than doubting, faith must be firmly clung to, and in faith you must persevere in your callings. You must act in accordance with righteousness because there will be an eternal difference in the coming judgment, even though punishments in the meantime are being meted out. Nonetheless, perform the duties of your calling even though much work will be fruitless or thankless. For at some point in the future, your labor will succeed. God will be present with the laborer and comfort the one who calls upon him. You should disseminate your teaching and your labors in faith "like bread being cast upon the waters,"[2] for by faith and hope you will alleviate any present anguish. In this way, Solomon prohibits our desperation and trust in ourselves while teaching us how to rest in God by faith. In fact, there is no other way in this life to relieve your sorrows, and any attempts to do so by other means or

---

[1] Source of quote unknown.

[2] Eccl. 11:1.

by abandoning society altogether is of no avail. These miseries cannot be avoided by seeking human wisdom; they can only be mitigated by allowing our hearts to rest in God in faith.

To this summary, rehearsing the various claims about troubles and consequences recounted above must be brought to bear, and responses are directly added. Over against these claims, Solomon establishes God's Word, the ordering of outcomes, and punishment for severe crimes as evidence of God's future judgment, which is, in fact, why he mentions this judgment so often. In fact, for every topic, it is important to consider the author's intention in writing, his meaning, and to what end he has arranged his work. In this way, we know that this book deals principally with providence. It then turns to consolation, knowing full well that the various misfortunes in life can lead us to doubt providence, forsake doing what we know to be right, jettison our everyday duties in life, and abandon our calling. These common consolations are drawn first from what is necessary, second from what is possible, and third from what is useful, that is, distinguishing between rewards and punishments.

First, when it comes to what is necessary, it is this: It is necessary to obey God. The assertion that God created the human race must be firmly maintained. And although it is true that difficult hardships routinely occur, we nonetheless firmly maintain that we will be preserved by God, that our labors will be supported by him, that he alone is our Examiner, Judge, and Refuge. This is why Solomon so often repeats these words: Let us fear God because God will judge all—whether good or evil, even what is hidden.

Second, when it comes to arguments from what is possible, it is this: It is evident that difficult hardships routinely occur, and the government is in many instances ineffective. As Solomon writes, "What is crooked cannot be made straight,"[3] and, indeed, even the righteous sometimes fall into error. However, in truth, God will not allow the labor of those who have been called to be completely in vain. On the contrary, God will be present with the one who calls on him. As it is said: "Cast your bread upon the waters,"[4] because you

[3] Eccl. 1:15.

[4] Eccl. 11:1.

will find him.[5] Likewise: "Plant your seed in the morning…"[6] Second, this consolation is frequently repeated—both here and elsewhere in Scripture. For instance, Paul says. "Your labor in the Lord will not be in vain."[7] And Psalm 1 states. "His leaf will not wither."[8] Regarding the topic of what is possible also pertains to remedies for sorrows. For instance, anger and great pain were ignited and burned in the bones of Pericles and other such leaders since their well-thought-out plans for the defense of the country did not turn out as they wanted. In contrast to these leaders, Jeremiah rested in God—even when things went against his way—for he knew that God alone offered the remedy, that God was to be obeyed, and that God would miraculously preserve his Church. As it is said in Isaiah: "I will always provide for you—even in old age."[9] Likewise: "And not even the gates of hell will prevail against it."[10]

Third, when it comes to the topic of what is useful, it is this: We must distinguish between rewards and punishments. For instance, not only are severe crimes punished in this life, but in the life to come, the Church will be adorned with eternal rewards while the wicked will be cast into eternal torment. This pertains to the third topic of Ecclesiastes, namely, the threat that warns of punishments on all who sin, including not only those outside the Church but also inside the Church. As it is written: "It will go well for those who fear God…but it will not go well for the wicked."[11]

Those are certainly the main topics of this book. Besides these things, Solomon also mixes in many comments about common occurrences and many virtues. Nonetheless, the entirety of his teaching in this book is concentrated under this heading: "Fear God and keep his commandments,"[12] which encompasses all worship, fear, faith, and good works. In this way, the admonitions of this book will

[5] The assumption is that the bread represents our prayers while the waters represent God.

[6] Eccl. 11:6.

[7] 1 Cor. 15:58.

[8] Psalm 1:3.

[9] Isa. 46:4.

[10] Matt. 16:18.

[11] Eccl. 8:12–13.

[12] Eccl. 12:13b.

prove useful when joined with additional teaching of faith, the true God, conversion or repentance, knowledge of the Son of God, the righteousness of faith, and new obedience. Solomon preaches this to members in the true Church, to whom God has revealed himself and delivered his promises. And therefore, the works associated with our calling are found pleasing to God, and the ordinary labors we perform are reckoned as our worship of God when our faith shines forth, through which we are regarded as righteous on account of the Redeemer, the Son, and it is through this very faith that we seek God's guidance and help. As the Lord has said, "You can do nothing without me."[13] Likewise: "How much more so will your Father in heaven give the Holy Spirit to those who ask him."[14] When faith rules over our works, at the same time it connects them to God's glory. For the worship of God is a work commanded by God, performed by trusting in the Son of God, the main purpose of which is that this obedience renders honor to God and demonstrates that we are invoking the true God, who has revealed himself in the Church. This faith likewise brings peace of mind because it subjects us to God, and it confirms God's presence in our lives as our Refuge and Deliverer. As Paul has said, "The peace of God, which transcends all human understanding, will guard your hearts."[15]

However, because there are so many varied principles [*sententiae*] that have been strewn throughout this book, prudence is needed when distinguishing among them. In fact, in all writings that contain principles, it is necessary to classify them according to their type [*genus*]. For instance, in sacred scripture there are many types: Law, Gospel, Doctrine, Consolation, and some are simply accounts of eventualities—good and evil.

Law is found in many statements frequently repeated with regard to our calling: "Diligently perform the labors God has given you."[16] And Solomon also joins threats to these precepts, as found here: "It will not go well for the wicked."[17]

---

[13] John 15:5.

[14] Luke 11:13.

[15] Philip. 4:7.

[16] Eccl. 9:10.

[17] Eccl. 8:13.

Statements of Gospel are such things as: "Whoever believes in the Son has eternal life."[18] In fact, these are connected to many other sayings about faith, prayer, and consolation embedded throughout the holy writings, for instance, "Ask and you will receive."[19] Likewise: "How much more so will your Father in heaven give the Holy Spirit to those who ask him."[20] And in this book of Ecclesiastes: "All should find satisfaction in their work, for this is the gift of God."[21] And even though this speaks more obscurely about faith, it nonetheless means that we must ask for and hope for help from God.[22] As it is written in Psalms: "Commend your way to God, and he will act for you."[23] This aligns with this saying: "Your labor in the Lord will not be in vain."[24]

Other statements concern doctrine, offering instruction about God's essence, providence, will, and judgment. For instance: "You shall have no other god before me,"[25] and "There is no other God."[26] And in this book: "God will judge both what is secret and what is revealed."[27]

Statements about consolation refer back to Gospel. For instance: "God is near those whose hearts are broken."[28] Likewise: "Call upon me in the day of trouble and I will rescue you."[29]

Accounts of eventualities abound in this book and include: "The wise and the fool die alike."[30] Likewise: "What is crooked

---

18 John 3:36.

19 Matt. 7:7.

20 Luke 11:13.

21 Eccl. 3:12–13.

22 Melanchthon's distinct *locus* method of biblical interpretation allows him to seamlessly connect here a seemingly random passage in Ecclesiastes to the heart of the Gospel.

23 Ps. 37:5.

24 1 Cor. 15:58.

25 Ex. 20:3.

26 Isa. 45:6. Note that there are several places in Isaiah—and elsewhere in the Bible—where this phrase is located.

27 Eccl. 12:14.

28 Ps. 34:18.

29 Ps. 50:15.

30 Eccl. 2:16.

cannot be made straight."[31] Also: "There is not a righteous person on earth who does what is right and never sins."[32] For this reason, it is prudent to distinguish such accounts from sayings containing decisions and promises, for example, "Fate makes a fool out of the one she favors,"[33] and, "Feelings run wild in prosperity."[34] And within this book, there is the following: "I saw wickedness in the place of justice."[35] Such accounts do not approve of evil. Rather, they demonstrate that we should consider them as warnings and be diligent to avoid them—in the same way a physician studies and classifies diseases.

I have spoken about these kinds [*genus*] of sayings in the prophetic and apostolic scriptures, so now let us turn to philosophical sayings. There is nothing of Gospel or Doctrine in these sayings. However, they do contain Law as well as accounts of eventualities. For example: "Do not trust the people, for the mob is fickle."[36] However, we must always keep in view that there are clear differences between the sayings of Hesiod, Phocylides, and Theognis and those sayings contained in the holy scriptures. As such, secular accounts are to be received differently than accounts in the holy scriptures. For example, it is written in one saying: "Life is governed by fate, not wisdom."[37] And in the saying of Solomon we read: "The race is not won by the fastest nor is food earned by the wisest."[38] But here is the difference. Solomon is ordering us to do right things in accordance with the divine commands, forbidding human curiosity lest, trusting ourselves, we be compelled to do that which is outside our calling. He also forbids us to trust in our own confidence in the works of our

---

[31] Eccl. 1:15.

[32] Eccl. 7:20.

[33] Publius Syrus, *Sentences* 271. This common saying circulating among the ancient Greeks. By way of note, his praenomen, or given name, is also spelled Publilius.

[34] Ovid, *Art of Love* 2.437.

[35] Eccl. 3:16.

[36] Pseudo-Phocylides, *Sentences* 95. In Greek: λαῷ μὴ πίστευε, πολύτροπος ἐστὶν ὅμιλος.

[37] Cicero, *Tusculan Disputations* 5.9. Cicero is quoting Theophrastus, an ancient Greek philosopher and friend of Aristotle.

[38] Eccl. 9:11.

calling, wanting us to seek God's help and obey him regardless of the outcome. Consequently, Solomon speaks in favor of providence in contrast to this secular saying which does not: "Life is governed by fate, not wisdom."[39]

There is a similar saying that comes from the life of Pomponius Atticus: "Fate is based on each person's character."[40] This saying seems to differ from another rule: "Many are the afflictions of the righteous."[41] However, this is a concession. The other saying is a political rule that is consistent with these sayings: Severe crimes are punished with severe punishments in this life. Similarly: "The one who takes up the sword will perish by the sword."[42] By contrast, the course of life is more peaceful for those who live temperately. There is an exception to this rule in the Church, however. For although God spares many who are weak, God nonetheless exerts more force on some. Of course, there are many established reasons why those in the Church are more burdened than the other people: It is because we must be conformed to the image of the Son of God.

The prophetic saying states, "Cursed is the one who trusts in humankind."[43] This is consistent with the notion of Epicharmus that epitomized and embodied[44] wisdom, for he said: "Remember to doubt."[45] In a similar way, Plato admonishes that hopes do not depend on fortune or human relationships; however, he says nothing about trusting God. In a similar vein, Cicero renders Plato's words in an epitaph in the following way: "People are of their own accord

---

[39] Cicero, *Tusculan Disputations* 5.9, 25.

[40] Cornelius Nepos, *Lives of Famous Men*, Atticus 11.6. The original Latin from Nepos's book is: *Sui cuique mores fingunt fortunam hominibus*, "Each person's character shapes people's fate." The Latin word *mores* is capable of multiple translations: "character," "morals," "temperament," "customs," "habits," "disposition," "values," etc.

[41] Ps. 34:19 (Vulgate 33:20).

[42] Matt. 26:52.

[43] Jer. 17:5.

[44] The Latin words *nervus* and *artus* were anatomical terms that doubled over as words indicating strength. In this context, however, I translate them as "epitome" and "embodiment," respectively.

[45] Lucian, *Hermotimus* 47. In Greek: μέμνησο ἀπιστεῖν.

suited to all things that lead to a happy life that is not dependent on others, good luck, or the opposite when compared to the best way of living."[46] Cicero rightly admonishes us not to depend on fortune or human relationships. Still, because he induces us to rely on our virtues, it is not enough. Instead, we ought to be led to rely on God, for there are many instances in which human virtue alone will fail us unless aided by God. And when all human wisdom fails us, God wants to be acknowledged and called upon, and he promises assistance. For the matter itself shows that calamities are diminished among those who call upon God. As it is said: "The Lord is near to the brokenhearted."[47] Likewise: "Return to me and I will return to you."[48] Also: "Though your sins are like scarlet, they will be as white as snow."[49]

The following two sayings seem to stand in contrast to each other. For example, while Ennius said that "fortune is given to the brave,"[50] Solomon wrote that "the race is not won by the swift."[51] However, there is a true resolution between them. Ennius's saying is scolding the cowardly while Solomon's is condemning trust in our own strength and neglect of God. Indeed, when David defeated Goliath, he was neither idle, cowardly, or careless.

In this way, it is necessary to consider carefully to what genre these dictums may correspond. And because the statements, for the most part, consist of everyday rules for life, it is useful to be very familiar with their content. In fact, because sayings also offer instructions for living, and because arguments, confirmations, and refutations arise in all circumstances, they also add weight to the prayer when humbly inserted at the appropriate time.

It is also necessary to consider the difference between a character [*persona*] and hyperbole. For example, Nero said, "The sword protects the ruler."[52] But Seneca responded, "Loyalty [*fides*] is better

[46] Cicero, *Tusculan Disputations* 5.36.

[47] Ps. 34:18.

[48] Zech. 1:3.

[49] Isa. 1:18.

[50] Ennius, *Annals* 257.

[51] Eccl. 9:11.

[52] Seneca, *Octavia* 438.457.

than the sword."[53] Likewise, there is a Greek saying: "All human matters are mad."[54] Still, such hyperbole should by no means be transferred to those things which are divinely ordained—for instance, to the message of the Gospel, to the confession of the saints, to the legitimate functions of the government, or to educational institutions. Here are some other examples of hyperbole: "There is no faith or piety among those in the military."[55] Also: "The Fates rule humanity, and all things stand firm by the Law."[56] Such sayings must be corrected through the filter of a learned and faithful interpretation.

---

[53] Seneca, *Octavia* 438.458.

[54] In Greek: πάντα ἀνθρώπων εἶναι μανιώδη.

[55] Lucan, *The Civil Wars* (also called *Pharsalia*) 10.407.

[56] Marcus Minilius, *Astronomica* 4.14. Note that the original Latin contains *orbem* ("the world") instead of *homines* ("humanity").

General Index

Scripture and Ancient Sources Index

NEW TESTAMENT

EARLY CHRISTIAN WRITINGS

GRECO-ROMAN LITERATURE

www.ingramcontent.com/pod-product-compliance
Lightning Source LLC
Jackson TN
JSHW020332050126
95842JS00003B/7/J

* 9 7 8 1 9 6 4 4 1 9 2 8 2 *